THE LOST
MAGISTRATES
COURTHOUSES

OF
YORKSHIRE

Raymond Charles Curry

This edition published in 2012 on behalf of Raymond C Curry
by Arbentin Books Limited
Christchurch, Dorset BH23 1JD

ISBN 9781906631109

A CIP catalogue record of this book is available from the British Library.

Printed by Berforts, Stevenage, Hertfordshire

Front Cover: The old Park Row courthouse, Leeds, courtesy of The Thoresby Society.
Back Cover: The old Ripon Liberty courthouse, courtesy of the Ripon Museum Trust.

CONTENTS

PREFACE

This book nearly had a sub-title of half way down the stairs , based on a parody of the words of A. A. Milne. Several magistrates who have assisted with information have remarked on the absence of retiring rooms in some old courthouses, so they sat on the stairs.

The project started as the result of a casual conversation with a colleague in North Yorkshire who was bemoaning the loss of court houses for local cases to be heard. The 1974 changes of boundary from the former three Ridings into four sub-divisions of the county, and bits hived off elsewhere, brought some parts of the West Riding into North Yorkshire, and so the task developed from there.

In North Yorkshire distances between courts are lengthy and not many of the punters enjoy local justice. The 2010 announcement of further cuts is unlikely to improve matters as the county is to lose further courthouses; those at Goole, Selby, Pontefract, Dewsbury and Bingley, plus Guisborough; a very sad fact being that Pontefract was one of the oldest sessions seats in the county, indeed in the country.

The work has brought me back into contact with old friends from my times in court, and has introduced me to others who have been inspired to accumulate a deal of information about their local courts. Without exception I have been listened to and provided with many bits of information, verbally and in writing, from so many kind people who are anxious to see that their local history is not forgotten.

I am very grateful for the interest and support of the Ripon Museum Trust. As The Yorkshire Law and Order Museums, they are notable attractions for all interested in social history. The three museums, covering the courts, the police, prison and the workhouse are outstanding examples of careful husbandry as they illustrate life not just in Yorkshire but more widely across the country.

With those few words of explanation it is time to introduce the subject in more detail.

R.C. Curry 2011

SOURCES
THOUGHTS
and
CO-OPERATION

One of the interesting features of putting together this book has been the readiness with which those approached have agreed to be of help.

Right across the board, from individual magistrates and staff to those in local government libraries and other official sources of records there has been an eagerness to assist. A number of local history societies and local newspapers have also been helpful.

Readers will detect that in some places the additional details are quite considerable, being due in many cases to particular local interest by an individual or group; although in some other cases the information is much more sparse.

As mentioned at the outset, the purpose has never been to try to give a total history of the system of justice in Yorkshire, but to record the premises from which it was dispensed, especially in latter years. My diggings have therefore been of limited depth, but I do commend to anyone who is taken with the idea that they will be fascinated if they want to try to unearth more about their own locality and be well rewarded.

To those who, in 2011, seem to feel that we must only move forward, I say that we should do so on a basis of solid understanding of our history and the reasons where we are today. Year by year people in various countries around the world seek to re-establish their cultural backgrounds which were lost in the various revolutions, global disturbances and world wars of the twentieth century.

A desire to live together as one big world wide happy family, if achievable, is laudable, but that should not allow us to lose our heritage or individual identities.

The British justice system has been the foundation for good law and order throughout much of the world, and despite the number of changes by politicians over recent times it still remains one of the best, and one of which we should be proud.

It is good, therefore that so many people are interested and willing to help record in an accessible fashion the background of our local magisterial justice in the towns, cities and country areas.

I am so grateful for the kindness shown to me in my search, and who knows, if this short publication encourages others to dig up more in their own back yard, there may be more of interest laid bare.

Throughout the book words are generally used according to the style in which they are referred to in the sources provided to the author, such as courthouse, Courthouse or Court House; likewise with police station and variants.

NB. In April 2011 Her Majesty s Courts Service was re-constituted as Her Majesty s Courts and Tribunals Service. This should be noted in mentions of the former throughout the book.

PICTURES

I am grateful to all those people who have so kindly provided pictures of court houses and other premises used as such, often with additional information, and these are all mentioned and accredited within the substantive text and at the end of the book.

In the event of any accidental omission or error, due apologies are given without reservation. In the event of further print runs such, if notified, would be rectified.

PRIVACY

The author especially requests that readers who get carried away with a desire to investigate further do respect corporate bodies and, in particular, the privacy of current private owners and do not intrude upon or inconvenience them in any way.

THE YORKSHIRE WAPENTAKES

First, let us consider the meaning of the word riding . This originated from thriding , an ancient Norse way of saying third ; hence the Three Ridings of Yorkshire.

The wapentakes were another derivation from the Danelaw which related to equivalents of the Anglo Saxon hundreds , which are the measure in most other counties in Britain.

At the places from which a wapentake might have taken its name, it was customary for the people perhaps to be counted or to give their assent by raising their weapons; hence the meaning of the word, being as it were, taking a count of weapons .

Connection with the names might nowadays be difficult, that of Skyrack (place of the Shire Oak) being fairly easy to understand. Others are more complex and those readers who wish to pursue this exercise in nomenclature must seek that knowledge elsewhere.

The entire county was geographically contained in these three groups of wapentakes, albeit within them two places were excluded. York was on its own as the City and County of York; the Vikings made it the capital of their Kingdom of York. Hull was founded by monks in 12th century and then acquired by King Edward 1st in 1299 to provide him with a port under his control, the Town and County of Kingston upon Hull. Nowadays, under a century or so of government legislation, both cities have become somewhat tangled with either the North Yorkshire or the East Riding administration.

The geographical logic of the division into thirds is not very complex to understand. The West Riding when considered on a map tends to follow the lines of the Dales and rivers which move from the higher reaches of the old Riding down to the middle around Leeds and Bradford. Even now, the cobbled up county of North Yorkshire has places which look familiarly to the west around Skipton, with the mid portions looking to Harrogate and Northallerton, and the eastern area tends towards Scarborough.

The North Riding tended to follow the lines of various valleys and tributaries towards the East/North East of the county, whilst the East Riding covers those parts inclined in that direction. The current South Yorkshire within the West Riding had the River Don which flowed to the Humber Estuary.

Although the wapentakes within the parts of Yorkshire are listed in each section, it may be helpful to mention here some of the main places within each of them. Wapentakes in *italics*.

Langbaurgh East and West cover the North East of North Yorkshire around Middlesbrough, Guisborough, Redcar and Yarm. Others in North Yorkshire are *Pickering Lythe* which takes in Scarborough as well as its namesake, and *Whitby Strand* which requires no explanation. Helmsley and Malton are in *Ryedale* wapentake, with *Birdforth* gathering Thirsk. *Allertonshire* is the area based around Northallerton, whilst further south *Bulmer* has a grasp over Easingwold and other places around there. *Gilling East* takes in Middleton Tyas, whilst *Gilling West* covers Richmond and into Swaledale. *Hallikeld* gathers in the Tanfields, whilst *Hang East and West* cover the area of Catterick, Masham and Wensleydale.

Within East Yorkshire, *Dickering* is the name for that around Bridlington, whilst *Buckrose* is more central, including Sledmere. *Harthill* takes in the various market towns from Beverley via the Weightons and Driffields to Pocklington. *Ouse & Derwent* are way over West based on Escrick near York, whilst the contra extreme is *Holderness* to the east of Hull. *Howdenshire* contains the town of the same name adjacent to the Ouse and the estuary.

West Yorkshire suffered badly from redistribution. From the former West Riding is *Ewcross* in the top most north west, including Ingleton and Sedbergh which has departed to North Yorkshire, as has the upper part of the *Staincliffes* next adjacent gathering in Settle and Skipton, but Keighley remains in West Yorkshire. Also despatched North is *Claro* containing Ripon, Knaresborough and Harrogate. Remaining in West Yorkshire is *Skyrack* taking in Leeds and its northern environs. *Agbrigg and Morley* contains the heart of West Riding industry from Bradford and the south side of Leeds to Wakefield via Dewsbury, Halifax and Huddersfield. *Osgoldcross* runs from around Pontefract to Snaith and Goole, so there have been departures to both East and North Yorkshire. *Staincross* taking in Barnsley has been largely lost to the South with *Strafforth & Tickhill*, which forms the largest component part of South Yorkshire gathering in Sheffield, Rotherham and Doncaster.

That whistle stop tour is not intended to be a geographically perfect treatise, just a familiarity course to assimilate places known at today with the ancient terminology. However, if that confuses, this excellent pictorial representation by courtesy of Colin Hinson of Yorkshire CD Books should clear up any locational doubts. Note that some wapentakes are broken into divisions or have isolated areas.

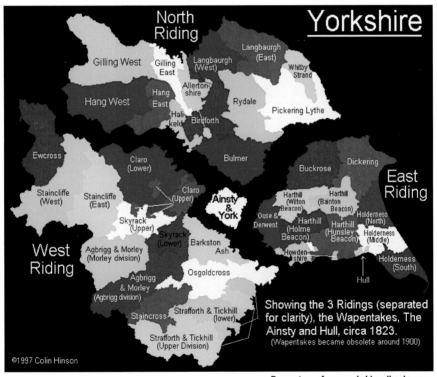

By courtesy of www.yorkshirecdbooks.com

3

ONE

Changing Times

I hope that perfectionists in matters historical will forgive me for the following potted version of court and judicial procedures in the centuries prior to now. It is intended to be an appetiser for the rest of the book, not an in depth review.

Readers who wish to delve deeply can turn to county archives and other repositories to do so. Likewise, those with specific interests in certain towns may wish to refer to their local sources of borough information to fulfil their hunger for knowledge, but I shall proceed.

Today there are far fewer courthouses than even just a decade ago. Those which are left may be very modern with every facility for magistrates, witnesses and defendants, all to comply with the various parts of the Human Rights Act and as required by legal statutes, access for the disabled, health and safety and many others.

It has not always been that way and even up to quite recent times some of the facilities for one party or the other have been less than appropriate. Some cells might have reflected earlier times than the 19th century when they were built. Facilities for interviewing the defendants were non existent in many courthouses until recently, and were often little more than the corner of a draughty corridor, where opposition witnesses were likely to be within earshot.

Such witnesses were free to be intimidated by any aggressive relations or friends of the accused and in far too many cases they were too afraid to give evidence. On leaving the court they often had to run the gauntlet of the guilty party s supporters.

Going much further back, we then have to consider some of the earliest court procedures, one of these being in the Anglo Saxon Wapentake of Skyrack, which met at the Shire Oak, now in Leeds at Headingley, but then a pleasant open country area with a large oak tree. Under this oak gathered the leaders of the district and, amongst their other duties, they administered simple law for the people. Such was replicated in other places across the Ridings of Yorkshire.

The remains of the ancient Skyrack Shire Oak stood on the Otley Road in Headingley, Leeds until 1941. Nowadays the names are retained in the two public houses set on each side of the road.

Picture kindly provided from his collection by D C H Hall JP.

The ancient tree survived until 1941 when it finally gave up the ghost on May 26th and fell. A new tree was planted, but that is still a sapling in comparison with the original.

As noted in the previous preamble there were many such wapentakes, derived from ancient Scandinavian meaning, symbolic of the hundreds into which so many other Shire counties were divided. The North Riding of the county was divided into thirteen of these wapentake units, the West Riding had fourteen and the East Riding had twelve.

Matters progressed in the following decades and centuries so that during the early and later Middle Ages buildings of various types came into the equation. Moot Halls, Town Halls, even coaching inns, and perhaps in some parts of the country, farmers barns contained some occasional courts . In these cases the magistrates arrived from the county Quarter Sessions bench. In some places the magistrate was a local squire who had miscreants hauled before him by the local law enforcer in the back room of an inn, or in a room at his house.

The range of various local and manorial courts largely and progressively reduced in significance, as the new magistrates' petty sessions and the 1840 national system of County Courts began.

The Municipal Corporations Act of 1835 had made changes to the duties of and system of appointing Justices which had been wide open to manipulation and nepotism amongst the upper echelons of society. It was still not perfect, but at least required appointment by the Lord Chancellor. Administrative powers were then just about entirely taken from justices in the new boroughs, leaving them with mainly law and order. Curiously, the last administrative duty hung on until the 21st century, removal of licensing matters to local authorities.

The vast bulk of the Yorkshire petty sessional courts were not built until those regular petty sessions began to sit in the 1830s. There was another wave of constructions, particularly in conjunction with police stations, in the late 19th and early 20th centuries. These were particularly evident in the East Riding.

However, providing a history of the magistracy is not the reason for writing this paper, as the purpose is to record court houses referring to the period from (say) Victorian times until the present date, 2010. During the last fifty years, especially within the last quarter century, the multitude of courthouses, some large and some very small, has been diminished to a handful, mainly in the major towns or cities.

Many older buildings have been abandoned by the courts to other purposes as new, functional, buildings have been opened. In Leeds, for example, the Victorian Town Hall had gradually been taken over by the courts, many of which were held in a variety of unsuitable and cramped rooms; some had even escaped into office buildings nearby. Since the opening of the new courthouse, apart from the retention of an original court and some cells as historical museum pieces, the building has been returned to the public in wider usage, although the Lord Mayor and City Council remain ensconced in the adjacent more modern Civic Hall.

The purpose of this book is to try to set out the list of all the courthouses, past and present, perhaps with a few anecdotes or historical facts to spice up the tale. All means all those which have been tracked down, as for certain there will be escapees from the net. The pictures may depict some which are much as they were when operational, but many will be in some modern guise, such as serving the community in a different way, as does the Art Centre at Thirsk. In some cases the purposes today are less sober, and more than a few have become places of pleasure, where drinking and dining are the main activities.

Please note, however, that it is not an attempt to write a detailed history of the individual courthouses, nor all that went on within them; that is a matter for more local historians, some of whom have done an excellent job; one very notable example being in Ripon where the Ripon Museum Trust under the guiding hand of Anthony Chadwick and colleagues, has done sterling work.

The details are intended to be even handed but, in some of the venues interesting matters came to light from local historical groups. It would be a shame not to include additional matter which brightens up the bare facts. In some places information was less profuse.

As a further comment, those who wish to learn more about the history of the magistracy itself from its earliest times should look for the detailed three volumes set entitled *The History of the Justices of the Peace,* written by Sir Thomas Skyrme, and published by Barry Rose of Chichester.

Also, please note that this is meant to be about the court houses within the old Ridings, although throughout this document the county location areas are being designated in their modern terms as North, West, East and South Yorkshire. Sadly, there are now some people in the county who may never have heard of the Ridings, as the current functional term now only relates to the East Riding.

It is interesting that the Local Government Act of 1972 gave notice that the changes were to create a *new administrative order,* not to abolish the old historical counties. However, the hard fact is that with the change the old order ceased, in practical terms, to have any relevance in modern Britain, and only purists keep the traditional names alive and observe the boundaries. Societies exist to maintain the names and history, and long may they continue to do so.

The courthouses which now lie outside the modern county in other counties may be referred to in some places, or may receive no more than a mention in this study.

When starting the project and enquiring around for sources of information it became evident that in some places others had trod before in seeking out the origins of their local courts. Sometimes this was in a fairly comprehensive form, in others more a collection of facts which had to be collated.

It will probably never be possible to ascertain in which public houses courts sat over the years, in the private houses of local squires or in farmers barns, or of the sittings held in local council chambers, libraries or other public buildings.

Some of these are mentioned, but it will be a fair bet that any readers going through the following patchwork of information will be able to say that such and such has been omitted. If that is the case, I ask them to try to make sure that these bits of our culture are recorded for the benefit of future generations. Some blank pages are provided at the back of the book for notes or enclosures.

Although history of our country does not seem to rank high in the instruction given in schools these days, and even then often only to criticise matters out of time context, it is our heritage. Across the world we see how nations which have suffered the anonymity of being repressed in the last century are seeking out their individuality as they look to make up for the lost years.

We may no longer execute murderers with a stake through the heart, but it is right that the vocal thinkers of the twenty-first century, when criticising harsh methods of punishment or restrictions amongst other cultures, do not imagine that Britain has always been so refined a place in its attitude to criminality or behaviour as it is nowadays. In 1815, a hitherto respected attorney in Leeds, Joseph Blackburn, for forging a £2 stamp on a mortgage deed was hanged at York, but it is fair to say that the over-all case against the accused was rather more complicated and involved, as discussed with the author in his more recent conversations with Geoffrey Forster of the Leeds Library.

For omissions or errors this writer apologises in advance, but the task of investigation is not over easy as in many cases it relies on personal memory from contributors, as official records of premises are not always as well recorded even if the court notes of cases may be in the archives.

I am however, most grateful to all those who have assisted in this project and the acknowledgements are listed in a separate place.

TWO

West Yorkshire

Although the modern county of West Yorkshire does not now contain the whole of the old West Riding it has not gathered in any pieces from other Ridings or counties. It has in fact been generous in parting with portions, albeit forcibly at the hand of the Government Boundary Commission of 1974 to North Yorkshire, South Yorkshire, Lancashire, Cumbria, Greater Manchester and to the quite short lived Humberside, now the revived East Riding of Yorkshire.

In respect of the old administrative and legal areas the Riding was divided into fourteen wapentakes

Ewcross The most northerly and westerly.

Staincliffe West. The next most north westerly.

Staincliffe East. East of Staincliffe West.

Claro Lower. To the East of the above.

Claro Upper. Mainly to the East of Claro Lower.*

Morley. Westerly, below Skyrack and Staincliffe East.

Skyrack Upper. Around what is now the Leeds area.

Skyrack Lower. To the East of Leeds.

Barkston Ash. Further East again from Skyrack.

Agbrigg. East and South East of Morley.

Staincross. South East of Agbrigg.

Osgoldcross. East of Agbrigg, spreading over to Goole.

Strafforth and Tickhill Lower. To the far South East.*

Strafforth and Tickhill Upper. The most Southerly.*

One other, Ainsty, was taken into York in the 15th Century.

These wapentakes had isolated parts within others.

It has been noted earlier how these wapentakes provided the earliest structure for the simple courts of local justice in the former centuries, but it is interesting to see how some modern administrative boundaries broadly followed the same lines for many years. This was also a guideline for the development of the local magistracy into benches until the considerable shake-ups of the late 20th century. The following representative map indicates locations of some known courthouses operating in the Riding before 1974 when boundary changes combined the smaller rural and urban councils into larger boroughs.

In addition it was not unknown for local magistrates to sit in council chambers, inns, schools or other premises to deal with work more remote from their normal seat.

West Yorkshire as a county in name is a result of the 1974 changes. Taken from it was the area which substantially created the new county of South Yorkshire, and there were shufflings around the borders with both East Yorkshire and Lancashire. The following map shows the overlay of West Yorkshire on the West Riding, and the balance of the West Riding which has now been despatched to North Yorkshire, but some to Cumbria as well as to Lancashire.

Most significant in 2010 are the locations of the courthouses now open and operating; few in number by comparison with those shown on the preceding map.

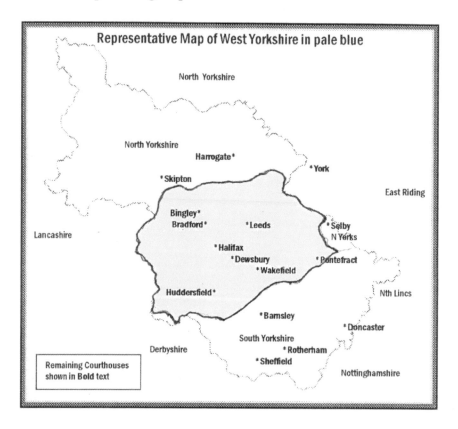

The ensuing notes endeavour to explain what has occurred in the former places over the years, some going back longer than others.

Leeds

Formerly a relatively small town within the West Riding of Yorkshire, Leeds developed rapidly during the industrial revolution.

Mention has already been made of the Shire Oak or Skyrack wapentake court which had a place in Headingley but affairs moved on from there over the generations.

Until the formation of the Leeds Borough by Royal Charter in 1837 which enabled it to have its own Commission of the Peace, the justices had been part of the West Riding Quarter Sessions which met in the old Moot Hall on Briggate. Even before then there had been a Rotation office, first in Call Lane, then in Kirkgate, both where the justices met to deal with administration matters.

The second Rotation Office on Kirkgate was the former home of Sir James Ibberson and was rented out by James Wood.

This picture, by courtesy of The Thoresby Society, the Leeds Historical Society, is taken from the marginal drawing on John Cossin's map of Leeds circa 1725.

The Moot Hall was located inconveniently in the middle of road, Briggate adjacent to Kirkgate, a rebuild in 1710 on the site of its predecessor which had been built in 1615. The courtroom was on the first floor and at ground level were the less magisterial premises of traders. Money for the construction of the Moot Hall had been authorised from funds due for poor relief on the condition that rents from the traders using the premises were directed back to the original purpose, but the bailiff of the day was less than open in this regard, and pressure had to be exerted to recover monies.

The Moot Hall, shown alongside, served as the courthouse until construction of the Court House on Park Row.

Picture in possession of and shown by courtesy of Brian Jennings Esq.

The Moot Hall building was eventually demolished in 1825, as its purpose had been overtaken by the construction of magnificent new accommodation. It also inhibited road development.

The Court House on Park Row, which is featured below, was built in 1813 and this fulfilled the task of housing the judges and magistrates for nearly half a century. In addition much other business of the borough was undertaken therein. The main room, adjacent to the courtrooms, held 800 people for public functions and there were thirteen cells in the basement. As in present times, costs overran the money allowed, so more funds had to be sought by a second Act.

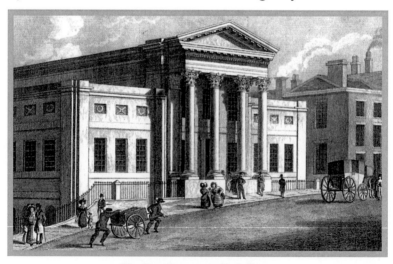

The Courthouse on Park Row.
Picture by courtesy of The Thoresby Society, the Leeds Historical Society.

The Leeds Court House on Park Row had been the subject of a campaign by many eminent citizens, and also from none other than the founder of the Howard League for Penal Reform.

Baines, in his 1822 work, mentions that the quarter sessions were held both for the borough and for the West Riding, and that a Rotation office within the premises was used twice a week for duties by the Chief Magistrate and an Alderman; this of course being before local authorities were created by the later Act of Parliament. Baines also refers in handsome terms to the other accommodation, the gaols and quarters for the military, including the armoury accessed through a guardroom. Times have certainly changed since then.

This building was vacated in 1858 when the Town Hall, designed by Cuthbert Broderick, was opened by Queen Victoria. The old Court House then served as the Central Post Office until, sadly, being demolished about 1903.

From that date onwards the Leeds Town Hall was central to the administration of justice in the City. It remained that way until in 1994 the new magistrates courthouse was opened on Westgate. The Crown Courts had previously vacated the Town Hall building for their own new courthouse next to the Town Hall, also on Westgate at its junction with The Headrow.

Leeds Town Hall.
From an old postcard in possession of the author.

During the course of its life as the court centre for Leeds both the Crown Courts and the Magistrates Courts were housed together within the Town Hall. In addition, the courts for the West Riding Division had been situated therein. The entire collection filled almost every room in the building and, apart from the main concert hall and associated offices, the main purpose had become the administration of justice in the city.

West Riding Court Leeds Town Hall.
Photograph copyright to and by kind courtesy of the
Leeds Library and Information Service.

The almost subterranean Bridewell and cells were a real relic of former times, and it was relatively late in the 20th century before they were brought up to modern standards.

Although this would be a great improvement for those who were incarcerated therein, it might not have appealed to those less concerned with any prisoner welfare; the hard hearted who talked of soft sentences being the ones with least sympathy for the offender cause.

Overleaf are comparisons between the Spartan style Victorian premises and the modern versions from the 1940s onwards.

The Victorian entrance to the bridewell is rather reminiscent of a medieval dungeon.

Picture from the Leodis Collection by kind courtesy of Andy Paraskos.

The 20th century version below is clinical but less forbidding.

Photograph copyright to and by kind courtesy of the Leeds Library and Information Service.

To the right, another shot of the entrance to one of the original cells shows another Spartan facility of the period.

Picture from the Leodis Collection copyright to and by kind courtesy of Andy Paraskos.

The modern alternative below.

Photograph copyright to and by kind courtesy of the Leeds Library and Information Service.

Across Great George Street behind the Town Hall and next to the Victoria Hotel there were additional courts used variously for family and youth matters.

Held in what previously were the West Riding Skyrack Division Courts from about the 1960s, when they had to vacate the Town Hall rooms due to pressure from the city courts, these have not survived, as licensed premises took over.

From the 1980s until the late 1990s, rooms were taken at 147 Headrow diagonally opposite the Town Hall to house the juvenile and later youth court matters. Several youngsters in custody were known to try to make a break whilst *en route* from bridewell to the courts. To say facilities within the city were stretched was an understatement.

Both pictures by the author.

That all came to an end in 1994 with the provision of the new court premises, built to Home Office specification, rather unkindly for a while known as legoland or the blue building, a hundred yards from the Town Hall, on Westgate next to the Crown Court.

As has been mentioned in the previous short chapter, various other courts had joined the Leeds City Bench by that time.

First after some local government re-organisation in 1974, the West Riding Skyrack Division which had sat in the Leeds Town Hall and at 26 Great George Street, Leeds, was broken up.

Horsforth joined in with Leeds and with Rothwell right up the east side of Leeds to Kippax and just short of Wetherby. That town, with the northern tip of the eastern area made up Wetherby Skyrack Petty Sessional Division, having first been deprived of Tadcaster which had been a temporary affiliation.

With this action within the new city boundaries the Leeds Outer Division was created, including Otley, Pudsey and Morley, all of the latter having been their own boroughs until the boundary changes in 1974 which brought about the new group.

After the further amalgamation of the Outer Leeds and Leeds City Benches which took place in 1990, these courthouses successively closed down; first Otley in 1997, Pudsey and Morley in 1999 and finally Wetherby in 2003.

Thus the business of all the magistrates courts in the Leeds district came together in the one building, and that will no doubt remain the case until politicians in government think of another idea.

The Leeds Bench, which had started with thirty justices in 1837 just before the early Town Hall days, had reached about 140 in Leeds by 1974, but by the time of the last merger into the one central body, there were some 400 on the list together with three full time District Judges (previously called the Stipendiary Magistrates) as well as some occasional visiting Deputy District Judges, the latter being practicing solicitors doing the task as occasionally needed due to pressure of work.

Before leaving the Leeds Courts it is worth recording that in the new court building hang the Coat of Arms of King James 1st of England and James 6th of Scotland. The history of these is that they hung in the Moot Hall at Leeds before being moved to the Town Hall when the West Riding Justices moved there.

At the time when the mergers took place the Arms vanished, allegedly into the care of a local worthy, but later they returned to their place in Wetherby (Skyrack) Court building. On the closure of that court house the Arms were brought to Leeds where they now hang in the archive area, but not open to the public.

The Leeds Magistrates Courts

Opened in 1994 followed the pattern of the earlier models of the new style premises which have swept the land during the last two decades.

Architectural comparisons with the magnificent Park Row premises demolished in 1903 are inappropriate.

Picture by the author.

Of course, in a large court, the incidents of humour whether intended or otherwise are legion; Leeds was no exception. A former defence solicitor Barrington Black, now a Judge in London, offered this one to the author.

It was in respect of a defendant who had no inclination to be remanded in custody, and Mr Black did his best for him. A request from the senior magistrate as to why the defence plea had been so strong, brought the reply that defendant really wanted to stay with his family. The reply from the bench was that he was certain to do that as he was going to be remanded in custody. Q.E.D.

Another example heard by the author was the solicitor who explained his client had been coming to the court for so long, that he remembered the last time the windows had been cleaned. This witticism appealed so much to its originator that he took the trouble to repeat it to the press representative who happened to have nipped out of court for a few minutes and thus missed the moment.

Then of course there was the slip of the tongue by the lady chairman who, on hearing that an indecent flasher had made his parade on the balcony of a multi-story flat a fair distance away from the female complainant, remarked that this would have to be seen to be believed .

However, the promise from the father of a troublesome gipsy traveller who had been given a warning by Binding Over, sent via the court clerk to the justices in their retiring room, that they would be looked after for their kindness never came to pass. In other words no offerings were laid on their doorsteps in the darkness of the night.

Such golden moments are the treasury of life in the serious atmosphere of the courts, and many a tedious day has been lightened by the expressions which pass, intended or accidental, between the various parties during the course of a magisterial sitting.

Morley

The early twentieth Century Prime Minister Asquith was a son of Morley and it is not unfair to say that the citizens of the borough always held a rather superior opinion over their rather flash modern upstart companion.

As already noted, the town dated back with a long existence in the Morley Wapentake name as did its neighbour within Skyrack, which has since eclipsed its position in significance and size.

The same could not be said of the magnificent Town Hall which was only opened in 1895, some forty odd years later than the one in Leeds. However, Morley Town Hall has been, and still is, a considerable and imposing building.

As will be seen, the latter story of the Morley courthouse is not unlike that of Pudsey. On the closure of the Rothwell court as a result of the 1974 boundary review many residents from that area who had to attend the Skyrack court in Wetherby did not have the means of transport to get there, so they were allowed to attend at either Morley or even at Leeds.

With the demise of the individual local authorities the same fate of the town dignitaries befell Morley, and within the Town Hall the court service gained another magnificent, if rather large, court room and an excellent retiring room in the former Council Chamber, as well as the original Number One court. Also included were the prison cells down in the lower depths of the building.

As with Pudsey the succession of events was relentless as the facilities for defendants, especially any in custody, and those for the other attenders were not up to modern requirements. The axe of closure finally swung in 1999, and another chapter in the life of the courthouses in the boroughs around Leeds came to an end.

The Morley magistrates had always been an independent lot and a number did not make the translation to Leeds bench. It is quite significant to this day that the Leeds City Councillors for Morley are entitled Morley Independents . Morley retains a Town Council.

There are some interesting snippets of information about the Morley justices, for which I am greatly indebted to Councillor Joe Tetley and the Morley Antiquarian Society.

From the 1977 manuscript of former police officer J C M Daniel come further instances of local justice, summarised below.

The Folk Moot (Peoples Court) was established in Morley in the first Century AD when the Angles settled in Morley. Later the Morley Wapentake was established and by the time of King Alfred the task of dealing with miscreants had devolved to the clergy at the Church of St Mary in the Wood. Offences could be as simple as failing to have a cup of water at the door for the use of any thirsty travellers, a fate which befell the Thane of Churwell in 626 AD who was fined one shilling; in those days a vast sum of money.

Later however, by 871 AD things were getting a bit brutal and some punishments would not have met the present day standards of Human Rights. Take the brawling in church offender who was to be nailed by his ear to the church door, or the murderer despatched with a stake through the heart and buried at the crossroads, or the debtor who was to be collared and sold as a slave.

Matters progressed, and by the mid 13th century some element of kindliness had crept in from time to time, in that one man who had assaulted two others was pardoned in the court in Wakefield *because he was poor'*. The interest here lies in the name of the complainants, Walter and William de Wodekyrk, it being plain that the two came from Woodkirk near Morley, whilst the offender John de Baggehyll must have hailed from Baghill at Pontefract.

Another feature of the local justice system in the 17th century was the ducking stool. Various dishonest persons such as traders who ripped off customers with poor weights or bad goods would first be towed around the town in a tumbril, and then be put on the long planks of the ducking stool before being ducked into the cold water of Morley Hole, or Flush Pond in Owler s Lane by Ratten Row.

In the early 19th century, prior to 1817 and well before the bench of magistrates being appointed in 1893 and courts being built in the new Town Hall, the justice of the day, one Watson Scatcherd JP, administered justice on Justice Day, usually once a fortnight, in the Nelson Inn, pictured overleaf, at the top of Victoria Road whilst sitting on The Jacobean Chair of Justice, later pictured, which is now kept in the Town Hall. The old court room in the pub, which was mentioned as the inn parlour, is not identifiable today.

When the Magistrates Courts were first established in 1837 Morley cases had to be taken in the Dewsbury Court, but that ceased in 1893 when the Morley Bench of twelve JPs was appointed.

In his book on Morley by David Atkinson there is a picture (below) which shows the Morley Magistrates, appointed in 1893, outside the Old Town s School where they first sat.

12 new Morley Justices of the Peace together with police officers - 1893.
Shown here by courtesy of the Leeds Library and Information Service.

Subsequently, after the opening of the Town Hall in 1895 they then sat in the courthouse in that building, and this continued to be the case until the courtroom was closed on 30th March 1999, and all business thereafter was transferred to Leeds.

Two of the premises which were previously used by the magistrates in their work of meting out justice to any of the more wayward citizens of Morley are shown on the following page.

Picture of the Old Town School at Troy which was used as the Court House
between 1893 and 1895 when the Town Hall was opened.

Picture shown by courtesy of The Thoresby Society, the Leeds Historical Society.

Between 1800-1817 justice was meted out in a room at the Nelson Arms,
where the magistrate sat on the Seat of Justice.   Author's picture.

Morley Town Hall opened in 1895 was a classic Victorian edifice with a fine council chamber and magisterial facilities.

However these did not meet the needs of 20th century legislators who required modern facilities, which coupled with the pressure from the government, brought about closure of the courts in 1999.

Author's picture.

The Clang of the Prison Door.

The Chair of Justice.

Some features of the Morley Courts.

Author's pictures.

Featured on the previous page, the image of the old cells and the almost medieval route into them for those brought to the court for the day, let alone held in them overnight, was sufficient for the local Magistrates Courts Committee to rule against their continued use.

Happily the seat, which in the early 19th century had taken the posterior of Watson Scatcherd JP when justice was meted out in the Nelson, remains in better condition and has pride of place in the room still used by the Town Mayor of Morley in the slightly lesser role of today within the enlarged City of Leeds.

Leeds has however honoured a Morley lady, Councillor Judith Elliott as being the Lord Mayor of Leeds in the mayoral year 2009-2010. Her husband was chairman of the courts committee of local magistrates which had the painful task of rationalising the courts in Leeds and West Yorkshire.

Morley Courtroom showing the original 1895.

Courtesy of The Morley Community Archive Group.

In 2008, showing the magnificence of the woodwork.

Picture by the author.

Morley magistrates continue to sit in the Leeds Courthouse, but unlike at the time of their transposition, when they mainly had Morley cases reserved for them in a Morley court , they now deal with all matters before the courts, just the same as the justices from the other former courthouses of the Leeds Outer Divisions.

The Town Hall continues to serve the locality in a lively way as the Town Council makes good use of its facilities and citizens of the former independent borough are well served by the various city services centred therein.

Revenue is gained by the renting of the courtroom and other parts of the building to television companies for dramas centred in the Yorkshire landscape.

The author is grateful to Councillor Elliott for her help right at the early stages of this book research being commenced. She was kind enough to make the introductions to those named above, who were willing to give the author access to the history room in the Morley library. In addition she effected the link to those in neighbouring Rothwell who likewise were generous with their interest and support.

Wetherby

Wetherby, as part of Leeds MDC, is discussed here.

Opposite the Swan Hotel on what used to be the main A1 route through the town, until the bypass was built, is Wetherby Manor, on the wall of which is a plaque which tells us that a court house was in the garden of the premises, but no dates are given.

Wetherby Manor

The blue plaque on the Manor wall also tells us that until 1824 Wetherby was owned by the old Cavendish family.

It was probably after then when the first court house in the Market Place was built.

Author's pictures.

It is not quite certain when a court house was first provided for the West Riding Quarter Sessions, except that in 1772 at those sessions in Wetherby it was stated that *'the court house was in a ruinous state and too small'*.

 Not much seems to have been done about this as it was May 1845 when a committee met at the *Three Masons,* when they agreed that it would beneficial to demolish the old courthouse in the market place, with the other adjacent chapel building, in order to provide access to build a new Town Hall, including a court room, with other educational and civic amenities on the site. So this courthouse which was demolished to make way for the new one must have superseded the one in the Manor House garden.

Matters must have moved far more swiftly in those times than nowadays as it was reported that the foundation stone was laid on 11th June 1845, the building evidently being completed by 1846.

However, Wetherby was not its own Petty Sessional Division in respect of magistrates, and it was not until June 1857 that the Wetherby PSD was formed as a separate entity.

Author's pictures.

The plaque text includes:
Wetherby Town Hall was built in 1846 on the site of the old Chapel of Ease. The ground floor was the Church School until 1895. Upstairs was the Magistrates Court until 1962.

The courthouse which was established in the Town Hall was vacated in 1962, when a new courthouse, in conjunction with a new police station, was built just short of the roundabout where, until the by-pass was constructed, the A1 had entered the town.

Occasionally, in order to avoid unnecessary travel, mainly on Saturday mornings, a licensed courtroom at Garforth Police Station was used to deal with minor matters and remands until cases could be taken in substance in the following week. Prior to 1974 this had been the habit of the West Riding Skyrack Division, as in Horsforth, but after 1974 it was Wetherby and Skyrack.

Wetherby, since 1968, had been with Tadcaster as one Petty Sessional Division, the Tadcaster PSD having joined with Wetherby in that year. In 1974, as a consequence of local authority boundary reviews the Tadcaster part went to North Yorkshire and Wetherby joined with the Skyrack Division to form the Outer Leeds Group of benches within the new city boundaries.

The village of Wetherby had grown in the period just before the 1939-45 war and in the years afterwards it became a fashionable dormitory for many people from Leeds who had made a success of their businesses. Thus, a large number of residents from the town retained a connection with Leeds, and it was interesting just how many Leeds City magistrates lived in the outer township. In fact, it would be fairly reasonable to say that in the 1990s there were more Leeds City magistrates living in Wetherby than were the number of town residents who sat as justices on the local bench. However, bearing in mind that the outer division included Skyrack, many magistrates were located around the various parts of the countryside and villages between Wetherby, Leeds and Rothwell.

Because of its position the Wetherby courthouse was ideal for the holding of some high profile trials where security was of major importance, and it was used for that purpose by North Yorkshire as well as for other out of district cases.

Nevertheless its routine work was affected as travel to the courthouse was not good for defendants from parts of its division, and most defendants could get to Leeds with far less inconvenience.

Latterly a large part of the lists in the outer court could be the bulked up paperwork cases taken from the whole Leeds area, such as basic motoring matters, many of which were held without any defendant attenders.

The final straw to retaining the courthouse as a financially viable unit died when the dreaded asbestos was found in the roof and ceiling voids. Its form may not have been the dangerous variety but alarm bells rang and it had to go. Cases ceased to be taken early in 2003 and that was the end of the era of the other courthouses within the old boroughs and towns around the Leeds area.

The 1960s Court building was typical of the period. It housed the police and when this picture was taken in 2008 they were still working from there.

Author's picture.

The tale does not quite end there as the formal consultations about closure of the premises did not commence until 2005, but they seemed to end inconclusively as ownership of the building seemed to be in doubt. It seemed that the land and original buildings thereon were donated to the town some long time ago.

That may be so, as the Wetherby Town Council now at least has some of their meetings in the premises - Court No 1 being noted in the minutes of meetings in June 2009.

Horsforth

Horsforth, a village, or some would say a small town, is set alongside the A65 trunk road from Leeds to Burley-in-Wharfedale, and onwards to Ilkley and Skipton. It has attracted a good population centred around its village. It classifies as an ideal local community. It was, and still is, proud of its independence from its larger neighbour.

Christopher Townsley, a Horsforth Councillor, recalls a few items of information in respect of former times. ..

"The only reference to 'Justice sessions' were recorded at the Old King's Arms and the Black Bull on the Green and the Stanhope Arms (now the 11th Earl on Fink Hill) and the village stocks were sited in front of the Old King's Arms and appeared to be still in use up to 1879 when the premises were extended. (These were a replacement in 1814 as the old ones had become 'worn out'). Total cost of the new ones - £3 for the ironwork, 3s. for the new lock and 3s.6d for selfwork".

The Old King's Arms above.

The Stanhope Arms, top right.

The Black Bull, bottom right.

Author's pictures.

Some time after this period the courts must have ceased to use the public houses, but it is not quite clear as to where they sat before the time in the mid 1900s when they were part of the Skyrack Division sitting in Leeds. It is known that until 1974 there were occasional court sittings on Saturday mornings in a room, above the new police station on the Horsforth Ring Road, which was licensed for that purpose.

A Leeds magistrate with some knowledge through a former Horsforth justice at that time recalls the use of a room which as described was the Council Chamber of the former Horsforth UDC, which now forms part of the first floor in the local town Museum.

The Council Chamber in the Horsforth U D C Offices seems to have been used, at least on some occasions, for the administration of justice.

Author's picture.

Horsforth had its own Urban District Council which was administered under the aegis of the West Riding County Council in Wakefield, but in 1974 local government re-organisation dispensed with the West Riding County Council and Horsforth became part of the city of Leeds, which had expanded its boundaries as required by the review.

The King s Arms and the Black Bull, together with the UDC offices all flanked The Green. The Stanhope Arms was about one hundred yards away. The seat of justice in Horsforth did not move a great deal over the years until its departure to the Skyrack Division Courts in Leeds.

However, by 1974, the local magistrates, as part of the outer Skyrack Division, had lately been sitting in the Skyrack Court Room in Leeds, so for them it was a fairly simple process of transferring to the Leeds City bench and sitting with all the other justices in the main court rooms.

The old Horsforth Police Station, at the top of Town Street where it has also been suggested that occasional courts might have been held, had been closed down and replaced with a new one on the Leeds Ring Road. Eventually that also ceased to serve as a local facility and its purpose turned to more specialised police work. It is no longer in existence as a local police station.

After the enforced amalgamation of Horsforth with Leeds the old police station was demolished to make way for a road which then formed part of a one way traffic system. The Mechanics Institute alongside survived and was refurbished with an additional section added as the Public Library, which it now houses, as well as some other local services.

Horsforth Mechanics Institute and Police Station on Town Street in the 1960s. The Police Station on the left was demolished to make way for the library which also includes part of the original main building.

Picture by courtesy of Horsforth Museum.

Rothwell

Lying on the south eastern side of Leeds between Morley and Oulton on the Wakefield road from the city, Rothwell is a small town which developed with the textile trade and, to a certain extent, mining, as it lay on the edge of that industry. It lies within the Lower Agbrigg wapentake.

According to Batty s *History of Rothwell*, Courts Leet and Manor courts were held in the Coach and Horses Inn. Previously these had been held in the Manor near the church, this having been provided by the Calverley Estates of nearby Oulton Hall.

Coach & Horses

The Coach & Horses Inn on Commercial Street, Rothwell.

View taken from a postcard, provided by courtesy of Councillor Chris Townsley, taken probably early 20th century.

The Inn has been now converted into flats and apartments.

In 1834 it is recorded by Batty that those held in the town lockup overnight were brought before the magistrate, Mr Blayds, at Oulton, but the more serious cases were sent to Wakefield.

Previously there had been a very notorious gaol in the Main Street, but this had been closed and those held were kept at Halifax.

Rothwell had its own Urban District Council and came under the managing hand of the West Riding County Council, but as with Horsforth it became part of the city of Leeds in the 1974 boundary review and courts ceased to be held in the town.

However, part of the very north of the PSD became attached to the Wetherby bench although a number of magistrates moved into Leeds as part of the Skyrack division. It seems that Morley also benefited from some case load, as some defendants had difficulties in making the journey from Rothwell to Leeds and they were allowed to apply for their cases to be heard at Morley.

The former Council Offices in Rothwell.

Author's picture.

The court in Rothwell was at some time held in the Council Chambers which still remain in use by the community in 2009 as part of the One Stop Centre, and to house various meetings of local town councillors with other community groups, and for similar purposes.

Otley

Another victim of the 1974 boundary review was Otley, a busy market town, sitting astride the River Wharfe on the A660 trunk road from Leeds to Ilkley.

It too became an adjunct of Leeds much to the irritation of worthy Otliensians, some of whom it is alleged after the 1974 review decided that a road sign saying Welcome to Leeds , situated on the new inward boundary on the A660 between Ilkley and Otley, was an unsightly appurtenance. There is no record of those citizens having been arrested and hauled before the local magistrates.

The Victorian courthouse, unlike in many other places, was a separate building from the other civic properties set on its own road, aptly named Courthouse Street . One of its remarkable features was the separate block of cells to hold the prisoners, all heavily barred and a challenge for any miscreant to break out there from.

Unlike the two preceding venues, Otley held out on its own, with its own bench of magistrates until 1997, when the Magistrates Courts Committee decided that, after consultation, it should close. It was felt that the property could not be modernised to suit standards, at least not within a sensible limit relative to the work schedule.

One of the interesting facts when considering the evidence about closure was that so many of the local crimes were no longer committed by local people, a considerable number being the work of criminals from a big council estate on the other side of Leeds. Why they should target Otley remained a mystery. Much of the other routine work was motoring, and the offenders largely lived in Leeds or Ilkley, or even further afield.

It was also found that although the Pudsey court was part of the same division travel thereto was almost a non starter, other than by car, so the attenders were required to travel to Leeds unless they requested otherwise. Thus the number of attenders at Pudsey was not much affected by the loss of the Otley court house.

On closure of the Otley courthouse on 31st March 1997, the magistrates transferred to Leeds, although here again a few decided to retire rather than move to a new home.

The old Otley courthouse is partly retained as a piece of the town s history, together with a cell. The former was used from time to time on television in dramas when a courthouse of the period was required, but this task has now moved to Morley. The latter is now just a wish that it could be used, with its companions, against some of today s wilder miscreants who disturb the peace.

As with Morley and Pudsey, Otley magistrates undertook the tasks of maintaining Law & Order very seriously as they had no wish for their citizens to be up in arms at a lack of interest. The justices in these places, as in all smaller communities would be well known to people in the town, who would not be shy of saying their piece in true Yorkshire fashion if proper order was not kept in the towns.

I am very grateful to Linda Waite, a volunteer researcher at Otley Museum, for providing information from earlier times.

There is knowledge that earlier courts were held in a court room on the first floor of what later became the Bowling Green Inn. However it had an interesting history. Built around 1757 by Nathaniel Aked as a court and session house it was after a while found to be inadequate, and the sittings moved to the Old Grammar School in Manor Square until the new Courthouse was opened in 1875.

She further advises that in the book Little Town of Otley by Harold Walker Pub.1874, page 16 he writes *In 1813 the Court and Sessions of his Grace, The Archbishop of York, Lord of this Liberty were held in the School.* (He is referring to the Old Grammar School) *The lower rooms were also, for many years, used as a Courthouse for civil and criminal cases, before the present building in Courthouse Street was erected. A relic of the Archiepiscopal Quarter Sessions held in the old Grammar School for many years is Gallows Hill, just below the Cemetery in Pool Road, where felons condemned by the Justices were hanged".*

This implies that the Old Grammar School had held the Liberty Courts from earlier times, whilst the county magistrates petty sessions were a later addition in the 19th century.

The return of Petty Sessions of 1846 by the clerk Henry Newstead refers to the venue for sittings to be the *...Court House, a spacious building a few years ago altered and repaired by public subscription* . Now, although this seem ed to be the building known as the Assembly Rooms in Bondgate, this might have been the Old Grammar School, as by then in 1825 the original Assembly Rooms in which dances and public gatherings were held, had become an inn known as the *Bowling Green.* That is, of course, unless a room had been retained at the Bondgate premises which could be used.

For the purposes of this document we shall assume that both these buildings are worthy of being listed as venues for courts to sit.

The Old Grammar School in Manor Square.
Colour printed postcard. Postmarked 1909. Published by H. Mounsey of Otley.
Picture provided by courtesy of Otley Museum.

The Bondgate premises are shown in the following picture, recently taken, overleaf.

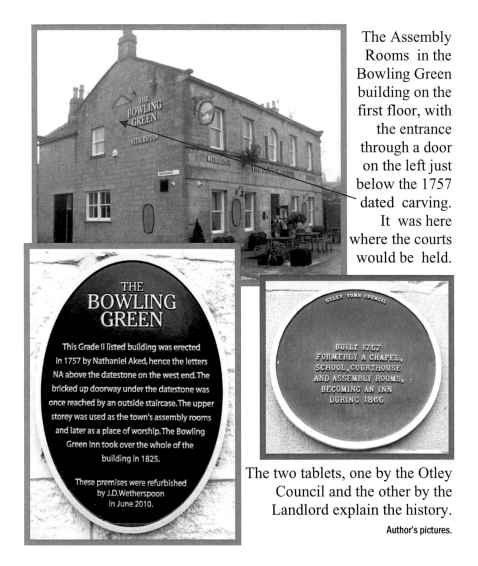

The Assembly Rooms in the Bowling Green building on the first floor, with the entrance through a door on the left just below the 1757 dated carving. It was here where the courts would be held.

THE
BOWLING GREEN

This Grade II listed building was erected in 1757 by Nathaniel Aked, hence the letters NA above the datestone on the west end. The bricked up doorway under the datestone was once reached by an outside staircase. The upper storey was used as the town's assembly rooms and later as a place of worship. The Bowling Green Inn took over the whole of the building in 1825.

These premises were refurbished by J.D.Wetherspoon in June 2010.

OTLEY TOWN COUNCIL

BUILT 1757
FORMERLY A CHAPEL,
SCHOOL, COURTHOUSE
AND ASSEMBLY ROOMS,
BECOMING AN INN
DURING 1865

The two tablets, one by the Otley Council and the other by the Landlord explain the history.

Author's pictures.

However, changes were afoot. The West Riding Constabulary was established in 1853 and in Otley this brought about construction of a house in 1854 for the Police Superintendent.

This was followed by the development of a courthouse on the site which opened in 1875, and those premises remain to this day. The following pictures show the extent of the buildings.

The Police House to the left and the Courthouse to the right.
Author's picture.

Author's picture.

The Prison Cells at Otley Courthouse used to be on both floors and some views of the interior are given overleaf. The modern lighting would not have been a feature when the block was built.

A cell at the court, toilet on the right.

The corridor to the cells.
Author's pictures.

Other views of Otley courthouse show the substance of the premises in what was, in essence, a small market town. They were, and still are, an important feature of the town.

The premises are now host to dramatic works and a variety of community projects which are of value to citizens of the town and of interest to visitors.

Author's pictures.

43

Pudsey

Pudsey was in Morley Wapentake and was part of Bradford until being made its own borough in 1900.

Pudsey only got its Commission of the Peace in 1909 but was part of Bradford Petty Sessions prior to then. Former magistrate Ruth Strong, who spoke to the author, had read somewhere about the justices meeting in an Inn at Clayton on the West side of Bradford.

This comment has been in part substantiated by Ray Clarkson a former member of the Skyrack Division who served at Bingley for some time. He comments that the Morley East area of Skyrack at one time had their cases heard in Bingley. Although the latter town is no-where near Clayton, it does confirm the Bradford link.

The Mechanics Institute, built in 1880, was converted into the Town Hall 1909-1910. The bench met in the Technical School whilst this alteration work proceeded.

As the other half of the Pudsey and Otley division, the two courtrooms in the Town Hall served this thriving township.

Despite the 1974 boundary review placing Pudsey within Leeds, geographically it lay much closer to the centre of Bradford. The Aireborough area, lying between Otley, Horsforth and Pudsey provided much of the catchment from which the various clients had to attend at Pudsey.

However, considerable housing estates were built on the West side of Leeds both before and after the 1939-45 war and some cases from these parts were brought before the Pudsey bench.

On translation of the borough power to the city of Leeds as the result of the 1974 boundary review, the office of Mayor technically became reduced to that of being a parish/town council leader. The council chamber and the mayoral room, alike with Morley, became sidetracked into usage as another courtroom and a high grade retiring room.

During the years before the court closure attempts were made to improve the facilities, and a fair sum of money was spent in trying to keep pace with modern requirements. The building was, however, never very disabled user friendly.

In addition, as with the other city peripheral courts, problems were arising in respect of security and the prisoner delivery service to the premises on days of court sittings.

Furthermore the facilities for the catering needs of attenders, as well as the staff and justices were sketchy, certainly not in keeping with the modern day requirements. The author recalls from a visit in 1976 that at 11am all business ceased, justices retired for coffee and participants to court business vanished into selected cafes, according to their status in the proceedings.

Although this improved somewhat during the 1980s and the 1990s, with continuing pressure being put on the Magistrates Courts Committee from higher authority to reduce establishments, and the limit placed by the council on funds available to further improve facilities, it was decided that this court should also close. This came into effect on 31st March 1999.

This picture of some of the former Pudsey & Otley magistrates was taken in the modern No 1 Pudsey Court.
Photographer Michael Brook, Court Clerk for many years.
Provided courtesy of Derek Middleton, a colleague.

As with Otley, most of the Pudsey magistrates transferred to the Leeds City bench, a few only chose to retire early.

Pudsey Town Hall on the left.

All pictures by the author.

The current name over the entrance at the rear of the building to what was the custody suite has a certain irony.

Magistrates used this entrance on the right of the building. The courts were on the first floor.

Bradford

Edward Baines, in his 1822 volume on the West Riding, does not wax at great length about Bradford. In his reference to the Piece Hall which was mainly used for selling the *piece* fabrics made in the town; its secondary use being as an occasional courthouse, stating that *'the general quarter Sessions of the peace are held there'.* This makes an interesting play on the two words, with their different spellings and very different meanings.

This picture of the Piece Hall to the left is by N S Crighton.

By courtesy of Bradford Museums and Galleries.

Old Piece Hall.

Reproduced by permission of Bradford Libraries, Archives and Information Service.

The double sided staircase led to the main room, probably where the sessions were held, more clearly shown on the sketch to the right from *Pen & Pencil Pictures of Old Bradford* by Wm Scruton.

The building, on Kirkgate, opened in 1773 at a cost of £1500 held the Quarter Sessions 1800-1834, being demolished in the 1870s.

By 1845, the Return of Petty Sessions for the East division of Morley, in which Bradford lay, refers to The Public Courthouse, no fee being paid for the usage.

However, before we get to that point, we must look at various other venues where courts were held in previous years.

This picture of The Old Cock Pit comes from William Scruton s *Pen and Pencil Pictures of Old Bradford.*

The building was actually a Methodist Mission House but was also used as a courthouse.

Reproduced by permission of Bradford Libraries, Archives and Information Service.

That was not the only earlier venue for courts to be taken, as the Sun Hotel in Ivegate, shown below, which had been built in 1741 also had a room for the holding of Quarter Sessions.

THE SUN INN, FOOT OF IVEGATE, BRADFORD

The Sun Inn.
Reproduced by permission of Bradford Libraries, Archives and Information Service.

Even this however had been preceded by the Court House in Westgate, a building set amongst a row of other properties and which continued to be used until 1797. This fairly ordinary building is shown on the next page.

The panel over the door to the left of the picture has the date 1678 and the initials of the Lord of the Manor, John Marsden and his wife. This was the doorway to the courtroom on the first floor.

The Westgate Courthouse.
Reproduced by permission of Bradford Libraries, Archives and Information Service.

However, the story of the Bradford Court houses does not end there as with the closure of the Westgate premises the sessions took themselves off to another room at the inn. In this case this was the New Inn on Tyrell Street, and a view of the premises from the rear showing the staircase to the Old Justice Room is next in this story.

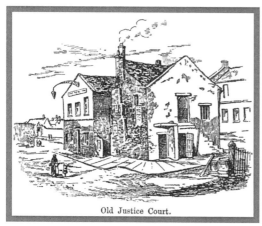

Old Justice Court.

Reproduced by permission of Bradford Libraries,
Archives and Information Service.

The rear of the New Inn showing the steps leading up to the court room and the cell underneath.

Sketch by Wm Scruton from the 1910 *Old Bradford* Series.

49

The Court House at Hall Ings was the next building which features in our journey. Built in 1834 at a cost of about £7,000 of which about half the sum came from the rates and half from local residents of Bradford, it really was the first serious dedicated building in the town; this of course having been brought about by the particular legislation which formalised the courts and sparked the 19th century country wide court building spree.

John James, in his *The History and Topography of Bradford,* published in 1841, having mentioned the costs, remarks . .. . *'In exterior it is surpassed by few, if any, of the Court-houses in the West Riding and internal arrangements and conveniences by none'* The picture below shows why it was so regarded at the time and it followed a similar style adopted in other parts of the county for court premises. Relatively few of these remain standing following 20th century demolition programmes to widen roads for traffic benefits.

Hall Ings Courthouse.
Reproduced by permission of Bradford Libraries,
Archives and Information Service.

This would be the court house referred to in the 1845 Return of Petty Sessions and the Hall Ings courthouse continued to be used for sittings of the West Riding magistrates who sat one day each week to deal with petty cases. The Hall Ings Courthouse was demolished in 1958 and the site is now occupied by the Telegraph and Argus.

The Bradford city magistrates, who were formed 26th July 1848 after the founding of the Borough Council in 1847, took their place in the Town Hall, as it was then called.

The Victorian architecture of the City Hall is in marked contrast with the 1970s style courthouse in the foreground.
Author's picture.

Bradford City Hall, Main Courtroom.
Taken by the author in 2011, by kind permission.

This lasted until the late 20th century when boundary reviews affected the position of the outlying PSDs which then all merged into one Bench in Bradford, leaving Bingley and Keighley alone outside the city in that area of the county.

The new magistrates courts were opened in 1972, not far removed from the City Hall, and that is where all the justices sat with the exception of the ones in the Aire valley who used the courts in Bingley, although this is to close resulting from a review in 2011.

The following picture shows the 20th century courthouse in all its pristine new 1972 glory. The City Hall is to the right, off picture.

Copyright - Bradford Museums and Galleries from image M014 from the C. H. Wood photographic collection.

Built at a total cost of £1,100,000 the 1972 building has eight court rooms for general use, half with docks for criminal cases and the other four to take the domestic matters or summons only cases. In addition there is a Youth Court as well as provision for Probation and Social Services.

The building also housed the Coroner s court. The main court rooms are centrally situated on the first floor with the various office accommodation predominantly surrounding them on the podium.

Another view of the Courthouse. In 2011 the water features
are gone as the area is scheduled for further development.
By courtesy of Michael Smelt, taken 2004.

The 'business' side of the City Hall.
The Courthouse is set to the left.
Author's picture July 2011.

Whilst considering the two buildings in the views above it is
also worth comparing the interiors of the premises. On the previous
pages is the fine and ornate Victorian courtroom in the City Hall. In
the 20th century, designs had become much more functional.

This picture of a main courtroom taken by the author in 2011 shows a sharp contrast of hard lined 1960-70s architecture with the highly decorative Victorian style.

There are two styles of courtroom in the 1970s courthouse

this is one of the smaller type with the lower picture showing some detail of the woollen tapestry coat of arms.

Pictures by the author
by kind courtesy
of HMCTS, Bradford.

As can be seen the necessity for natural light seemed to be far less important, with many courtrooms only having artificial lighting to illuminate the proceedings.

Announced in 2009 is that there is to be a new Magistrates Court built adjacent to the Crown Courts, and that the 1972 buildings will be swept away in favour of a lake to allow for other development, all of this being part of the plan to regenerate the heart of Bradford.

By courtesy of Janet Bunn, Project Officer for HMCTS, and the design team at Hurdrolland Partnership, the following images of the proposals for the new building are shown here to excite interest. The Magistrates will have the main accommodation, but the premises will also hold a Coroners court and two Crown Courts. Of course, as is the way of things, it may all change again before any foundations are laid. The site is between Vicar Lane and Bridge Street not far from the Law Courts, which flank the other side, and the Victoria Hotel.

On the left is the envisaged main frontage.

Both pictures by courtesy of the Hurdrolland Partnership.

To the right is the view as proposed from Vicar Lane.

In preparing this compilation I am extremely grateful for the help given to me at the outset by Michael Smelt, who for many years has been associated with the courts service in the city.

His interest brought to light the pictures hiding in the archives and I am grateful to the Bradford Library and the Museum and Gallery authorities for the kind permission to include them in this publication. Without the assistance given by Michael and so many other people this work would have been much more difficult to prepare.

Low Moor

James Parker s 1902 history of the Township of North Bierley, including Low Moor, describes the historic Royds Hall and includes ..

The Old Court of Squire Leedes still exists at Royds Hall, the broad flight of stairs leading to the room is significant of its former use and the 'Justice Chair' and canopy in the right hand corner still remain to avouch this primitive courthouse. Many curious stories of the Squire's mode of administering justice still linger in the folklore of the neighbourhood".

The late Jane Gummer, in her letters to the author related that her uncle Harry Sugden lived at Royds Hall, seen here in its still stately grounds. More recently the Justice Chair was not in evidence when the property was being marketed.

Picture by courtesy of James England, Carter Jonas, Huddersfield Office.

Keighley

Information provided by Ian Dewhirst MBE, a local archivist, notes that in the records of a parish constable between 1815 and the mid-nineteenth century there were many references to wrongdoers being *'taken before Mr Brigg'*, so it seems that the said gentleman was the magistrate of the day and possibly held court in his home, or maybe at times in a local Inn. Such practices had been commonplace, as will have been noted by readers, in other parts of the county.

Baines is silent on the matter, but the Return of Petty Sessions for 1845 notes that cases at Keighley were held for the extremities of the Skyrack, Morley and Staincliffe East Divisions, and such were transacted at the Court House belonging to the Court of Requests for a fee of 5s; the clerk being a Richard Metcalfe of Keighley. A County Court was built in 1831 on North Street but it seems that did not house the magistrates.

However, by 1887 a new Magistrates Courthouse and Police Station was built in North Street opposite the County Court and it is those premises which survived in use until the conditions imposed by the Government brought about its closure in 2000-01, as it failed to fulfil the needs of a modern society. The Keighley Bench transferred to the courthouse in Bingley and continues to adjudicate there.

The former Magistrates Court and Police Station on Northgate, Keighley.
Picture taken by the author in 2009.

Bingley

Records show that a Bingley Court of Requests was built in Myrtle Place in 1831 and that this was followed by a Police Court House in the same street in 1860 s, built on the site of the old workhouse, and the records show that the court was still in the same location in 1884.

In *Bingley - A Yorkshire Town Through the Centuries,* author E.E.Dodd notes *"Petty Sessions of the county justices had been held, no one knew how long, at Bingley, but there was no courthouse and the justices sat in any room available. Down to 1853 Bingley township belonged to the Upper Skyrack Division but in that year it was included, with East and West Morton, in a new Keighley Division, Wilsden being added four years later".*

He also mentions that that a Court of Requests was held in the King s Head Yard, off Myrtle Place, with a lock up adjacent. The buildings were condemned and in 1861 there was much concern in Bingley that the courts would go to Keighley.

As a result some money was raised and the police station with courtroom was built in Myrtle Place, in the 1860s, and the court sat there for at least sixty years.

He quotes *"...in a protest signed by some five hundred Bingley citizens, against the proposed transfer to Keighley....they combined a new suggestion. The old Bingley Workhouse had been officially condemned in 1857 and at last in 1860, the new Union workhouse at Keighley was ready and the Bingley paupers were transferred to it. It was proposed that the site of the workhouse and lock-up, which was also out of use, should be acquired by the county justices......and a courthouse and police station were built at the expense of the county, close to the disused court of requests building".*

This must have been very convenient for one magistrate, Lieutenant General Twiss who, according to Baines, lived in Myrtle Grove in 1822.

Myrtle Place about or pre 1850.

These two sketches from old prints seem to show the scene before and after the replacement of the court of requests by the new police station and court house. In the upper picture it is not defineable which would be the premises mentioned above.

Myrtle Place after the 1860s.

However, the lower picture clearly shows two buildings to the right of the shop on the left, one of which would be the police station and the other the court premises. Note the new lodge in the centre.

Sketches by R A Curry.

It is somewhat ironical that in the 1860s the people in Bingley were concerned that they would lose their courthouse to Keighley, as in the 20th century the reverse has happened with the business of the latter town more recently being held in the Bingley courthouse.

Ray Clarkson, who was on the court staff for a period in more recent times, recalls some changes to the present buildings when the offices were temporarily moved into the former police inspector s house. From much earlier times he recalls being told that the justices used to sit in the Brown Cow , an inn down by the river.

The Brown Cow in 2009 probably has more signs than in 1845.
Author's picture.

This is quite correct as in 1845 the Return of Petty Sessions says that the sessions were held in The Brown Cow, and that no fee was paid as the *'custom brought to the house'* was regarded as ample recompense. The expression in the quotation above that they sat *'in any room available'* seems to be confirmed.

Author's pictures.

Above is a view of the present courthouse on Bradford Road.

Modern extension now the public entrance.

The modern courthouse on Bradford Road in 2010 now in use was first opened in 1929 and, as has been noted earlier, carries out the work of both the Bingley and Keighley communities, each sitting as a separate bench. Thus press reports refer to matters being brought before the Keighley Bench, even though it sits in Bingley.

The area covered by the Bingley court included the parishes of Bingley and Ilkley and such parts of Bradford within three miles of Bingley.

As these words are being compiled it has been announced that the Bingley court premises will be closed under further government need to cut the costs of the justice system.

It is somewhat ironical that the concerns of the 19th century citizens about needing local facilities for the magistrates jurisdiction have now come to pass in the 21st century.

Slaidburn

It is at this point that this village, historically included in the West Riding, is inserted, albeit it has now the pleasure of being part of that other Red Rose county further to the West. It is of course much further northwards, and more adjacent to such as Skipton, but as it is no longer in Yorkshire, its demise as such is noted here, not in the North Yorkshire section.

I am obliged to Stephen Carter, an *émigré* from the county living in London, for the following brief notes and the pictures.

The village inn, the Hark to to Bounty served as a courthouse in past times, so says Stephen quoting *"..just over the border in that other county is a pub called Hark to Bounty in Slaidburn".*

"The first building on the Site was in the 1300s but the majority of the fabric now is from the 16th century, but there is a room on the first floor which used to be a medieval courthouse. I was there many years ago and went upstairs and took pictures".

Happily those pictures have been found and they adorn these pages. Thank you Stephen!

Calderdale

The name of the present bench of magistrates serving in this area may be an introduction of recent times on the occasion of the major boundary review in 1974, but it truly reflects the area which is covering the former boroughs of Brighouse, Halifax and Todmorden, all of which courts were combined into the one building in Harrison Road, Halifax in 1993.

The courts which sat in those places had done so for some years, but that is not to say that from time to time, as elsewhere in Yorkshire sittings of justices may have taken place in public houses, other council buildings in some of the in-between towns, or in some private houses of local squires. Church halls and some schools provided other venues albeit not always recorded.

More will be disclosed in the individual pieces about each location, but if any places where courts have been held are not mentioned that is solely due to the inability of the author to unearth more information from likely sources.

Halifax, the principal borough in the area, was in fact under the control of the Manor of Wakefield in the 12th century and the matters of justice were dealt with by the travelling Court Leet; but by the mid 15th century Justices of the Peace and Quarter Sessions had been established.

This was, of course, the pattern throughout the land as a more structured way of dealing with local judicial matters took over. Nevertheless, although the justices were appointed in order to bring some conformity to the system, they seemed to retain a deal of individuality which was not wholly reined in until the establishment of magistrates courts in the 19th century, and developed from then on. The courts today are a natural progression from those times.

As will be seen, Halifax and the Calder Valley area were no exception to this state of affairs.

Queensbury

Situated in Calderdale Borough but set on the hills towards Keighley, almost equally distanced from Halifax and Bradford, one slightly unusual court is listed as being located at Queensbury.

I am obliged to Derek Paley for the information that Nos 58 and 60 Catherine Slack (Halifax Road, west side) were used as magistrates courts in the very early 1800s by Michael Stocks of Catherine House. The premises are included on the English Heritage list as being of special interest.

This fine picture of the old Courthouse at Catherine Slack,
taken in 2005 by Derek Paley, is shown by his kind permission.
© Derek Paley

In addition Michael Smelt remarks, *When Michael Stocks of Catherine House at the head of the Shibden Valley became a magistrate in 1809 he was able to sit on his own 'Justice in Quorum' and used both the building at Wards End (in Halifax) and property near his own house to dispense justice, reputedly using the cellar as a lock up if it was needed".*

It is not known when that usage ceased.

Halifax

The present court building in Harrison Road was constructed on the site of the old Halifax Infirmary and the Assembly Rooms, and it was completed and opened in 1900. At the time it also housed the Police Offices, but they closed in 1984. The available space over the next couple of years was converted to additional courts and facilities so that the premises are now solely used by the justices.

However, as well as the Borough Courts there were previous courts in the town. Until the amalgamation in the 1970s the West Riding Courts sitting in Halifax dealt with work in the various Urban and Rural council districts other than Todmorden, and Brighouse after 1898 when it was given its own Bench.

Going back in history, there was a Moot Hall which was in use in the 13th century, in which the Courts of The Manor were held.

Halifax Moot Hall
Picture by courtesy of Malcolm Bull and the Calderdale Companion.

The building, situated close to the Parish Church, first made in timber but later faced with stone, survived until demolished in 1956-7; a tragic loss of such historic premises, but sadly not uncommon in that period when so many historic buildings were demolished.

For a few years around 1805 they utilised premises at Wards End, but it was not unknown for one magistrate to hold sessions nearer to his own home in the Shibden valley, as did others.

Premises at Queensbury were mentioned on an earlier page.

Picture by courtesy of Michael Smelt.

It is also on record that the Talbot Inn in Woolshops served the purpose on a number of occasions from the period onwards from 1804.

The Old Talbot Inn.

At the junction of Square and the Woolshops in which sessions would have been held. Demolished in the 1920s.

Picture from an original etching/sketch by Cuthbert Crossley, shown by courtesy of Stephen Gee

The habit of holding court in public houses, or inns as they were called at the time, was commonplace throughout England and really brought home the courts to the people.

One wonders how the idea would be received today with all the political talk of people s courts .

It is then recorded that hearings of West Riding justices were taken in a building on Union Street which had opened in 1818. This was actually the County Court and it was also used for the Court of Requests. In those times much of the work would have been relating to administrative rather than criminal matters.

Premises of the former Halifax County Court on Union Street.

Picture from
Round and About Old Halifax
by courtesy of
Stephen Gee.

When the Halifax borough was first established in 1832 a single magistrate, who also happened to be the Mayor, used an old workhouse building adjacent to the Parish Church.

As a stop gap measure between their appointments and the building of the Town Hall, the borough justices, thirteen of them in 1832, were housed in what was then the temporary Town Hall at the corner of Union Street and Westgate.

Site of the temporary Town Hall taken in recent years. The building remains despite the time since it was used for that purpose.

Picture by courtesy of Michael Smelt.

When the Town Hall was opened in 1863 it was noted the magistrates had use of a courtroom in that building.

In fact this was a substantial chamber immediately adjacent to the main hall in the centre of the building.

This picture was taken by the author in 2009.

As time progressed into the 19th century and following the establishment of Magistrates Courts by Act of Parliament, there was a specific courts building programme.

In Halifax the project was carried forward with notable premises appropriate to the status of such an important and wealthy town.

This is a picture of 11 Harrison Road, which was recorded in 1859 as temporarily being used by West Riding Magistrates until they moved to accommodation in their new Court House on Prescott Street.

Picture taken by David Griffith in 2009
Shown with his permission.

A County Court House on Prescott Street was opened in 1874 and more will be said about that later on.

The West Riding Court House was built on Prescott Street in 1889, and this housed the justices for the outer UDC and RDC areas.

The Prescott Street West Riding Courthouse.
Picture by courtesy of David Griffith.

Meanwhile, the Borough magistrates got a new home of their own, albeit with a Police Station attached. This was on Blackwall and the premises opened for business in 1898/99.

The Blackwall Borough Magistrates Courts entrance.
Picture by courtesy of Michael Smelt.

The local government boundary reviews in 1974 brought more change and the Calder Bench was created by the merger of the

West Riding and Borough justices in 1977, although both premises were to remain in use for some time. The police station shared usage of the Halifax Borough Courts until mid 1980s when a new Station was opened in Richmond Close. The Borough Courts then closed for a whole year for refurbishment and, technically at least, the justices all sat in Prescott Street which had been adapted to take them.

However, it was not as simple as that and use had to be made of the neighbouring County Court just along Prescott Street on the corner with Portland Place. This was not unusual as sources in Halifax say that such usage had been accommodated in the past from time to time. This merits the County Court appearing in these pages.

The rather handsome County Court premises helped out to allow the magistrates use of a spare court when needed.

Picture courtesy of Michael Smelt.

The Harrison Road premises, which also front on to Blackwall, were re-opened in 1987 by Prince Charles and the whole of the Bench moved back, vacating the premises on Prescott Street. These were sold off in later years to be redeveloped as flats.

At that time the courts in Todmorden and Brighouse borough areas were still each operating in their own rights. More will be said about these in the next sections. However they closed in December 1992.

On 1st January 1993 these were merged with the Calder Court into the modern Calderdale Bench which sits in Harrison Road.

This picture presents a view of the historical Harrison Road premises which now house the Calderdale Courts.

Picture by courtesy of Marian Griffith and Calderdale Court Archives.

It can probably be fairly said that the magistrates in Halifax certainly, whether serving the West Riding outer area or the Borough itself have had a fair journey over the last couple of centuries.

What started all those years ago as a piece of the Manor of Wakefield developed during the years of the Industrial Revolution and thereafter into a considerable power in its own right. Imposing Victorian buildings replaced the less robust predecessors, and unlike many others, have thankfully survived the possibility of attention by demolition experts before protection of our cultural and architectural heritage became the rule.

In preparing this short piece, the author is very grateful for the use of papers and pictures provided by Michael Smelt who has shown much interest in the courts in both Halifax and Bradford. For some years he worked in the Bradford Crown Courts.

In addition Marian Griffith, lately of the Calderdale bench, has been of considerable additional assistance in making sure that so many of the queries put to her have been properly answered to the best of her knowledge, and of any colleagues who have aided her.

It would be wrong to leave Halifax without a glimpse of two parts of the town s history showing the fate of some offenders. The lock up shown to the right below is at Heptonstall. It was one of six in the Halifax district.

This one was at the rear of a pub, Marian Griffith telling the author that the landlord supplied food to the prisoners.

A Halifax district 'lock-up'.
Picture by courtesy of David Griffith.

The Gibbett (reconstruction).
Picture courtesy of Malcolm Bull and
the Calderdale Companion.

In respect of the gibbet, Edward Baines delivers at some length on the matter. It seems that around the 16th century this was a main way of dealing out justice in the town, albeit that at times there was some lack of impartiality in the determining of cases.

The Bailiff was required to deal with such matters, and used to recruit four frithburgers to sit with him to adjudicate on the case. This seems to have been a fairly rough and ready approach and any who were found not guilty of the offence were released. However, for those whose guilt was established the result was arbitrary, and off with his head was the outcome.

The gibbet, as can be seen, was the forerunner of the French guillotine, and did its work swiftly and surely.

Around the mid 17th century the bailiff was instructed to cease the practice, which had been the custom for about three hundred years.

Brighouse

It is not clear without delving very deeply when courts first began to sit in Brighouse, but there is a record of the magistrates sitting in what was then the Town Hall, but latterly known as the Civic Hall, shown alongside, between 1898 and 1906.

Picture courtesy of David Griffith.

From 1906 until 1938 the courts were held in what was then the old Borough Clubhouse on Briggate, which has been demolished.

Brighouse Magistrates Courts 1938 – 1993.
Picture by courtesy of David Griffith.

Since then, until closure in 1993 the Court shared the above premises with St Paul s Sunday School until that closed in 1949. They are now known as the Salvation Army Citadel.

Todmorden

Life in Todmorden seems to have been simpler from a court point of view than in its neighbouring Calder Valley boroughs.

For many years, as noted in the 1845 Return, the court sat in the White Hart Inn, or the Golden Lion, or in a solicitor s office, that of William Eastwood, Clerk to the Justices.

The Town Hall was built in 1875, where the magistrates continued to sit until the merger with Halifax and Brighouse in 1993 to form the Calderdale Bench sitting only in Halifax.

The magnificent Todmorden Town Hall.
Picture by courtesy of David Griffith.

Kirklees

This generically named area now comprehensively covers all towns around and between Batley and Dewsbury and all the way to Holmfirth and the other outer parts of Huddersfield, as the latter 20th century invented, albeit historically named, unitary authority is all encompassing in the district.

Originally within the Manor of Wakefield the area developed its various towns during the Industrial Revolution, notably in cloth production from the wool resources of the county, although there was a significant development of engineering.

As will be shown on the ensuing pages, court houses remain in Dewsbury and Huddersfield but any others have been closed, Batley being the last example of an element of independence, which closed in 1989.

The area had Borough courthouses related to the main towns, but for a long while, until the 1970s, as in other parts of the county, there were West Riding courthouses as well, which covered various urban districts in between. There may, over the years, have been other venues such as occasional use of neighbourhood inns, and where any of these have emerged in the collecting of information from various sources they are mentioned.

As with other parts of the county, the author is indebted to a splendid mixture of magistrates, retired and serving, court staff and a number of local historians and community groups for the matters which have emerged and are recorded in this next section. No doubt there will be more available from digging deeper, but that can be the joy of others to find.

The best way to examine the situation is to move on to the individual towns and try to relate their courthouse histories.

Huddersfield

The 1845 Return of Petty Sessions has an interesting entry in respect of the venue for the magistrates in this part of Upper Agbrigg Division. Two clerks, a Mr Laycock and a Mr Bradley, verify that cases are taken in a room in the Guildhall which belonged to and had been built by a Mr Joseph Kaye, paying £40 a year to that gentleman for the use. In between court usage Mr Kaye let the room for other purposes.

In his book *The Story of Huddersfield,* Roy Brook says *"At the corner of Bull & Mouth Street and Victoria Street was the prison and the watch house, with the Guildhall facing them, (to the rear of Ramsden Street Chapel) used as a magistrates court."*

In this picture the Guildhall is shown to the right but by then, in 1934, it had been translated into a walk round establishment.

The larger print gives a better image of the Guildhall.

Pictures by courtesy of
Kirklees Images Archive.
www.kirkleesimages.org.uk

76

The period when the building was used as a court seems to be questionable, but being built about 1838 it was certainly used until Princess Street courthouse was opened in 1848, although according to David Griffiths there is a mention of Sessions being held in the Guildhall in 1857. Why that was so is not known.

David Griffiths lately wrote to the author *"I've now resolved the question of transition from the Guild Hall to the new court building in Princess St. Although the Princess St building is dated to 1847, it did not house petty sessions until December 1858, when a new court room was provided there, 'to the rear of the county police station and over the prisoners' cells'; this was opened and heard its first cases on 18/12/58 (*Huddersfield Chronicle, 4/12/58, 24/12/58). *Until then sessions were held in the Guild Hall; presumably the loss of his 'anchor tenant' led Joseph Kaye (or in fact his trustees, as he had died in March 1858) to sell the building to Ramsden St Chapel, as previously noted"*.

It is also known that the George Hotel, in the square of that name next to the station, might have been used but there do not appear to be any records of that on those premises.

This picture of the George Hotel taken by the author in 2009 shows its imposing location in an important position in the town.

The magistrates would certainly have found it to be a convenient venue.

David Griffiths and Brian Haigh of the Huddersfield Local History Society have been very helpful to the author in providing information about these above noted events and a timescale of the premises used for courts purposes, saying .

"The magistrates certainly met in the George (in the Market Place) at an earlier period, but we don't know whether they held

courts there. They also had an office in Market Street by the 1820s, where the magistrates' clerks and high constable for Upper Agbrigg were based".

"Later, the magistrates met in the Guild Hall, which was in Bull and Mouth Street, behind the Ramsden Street Chapel (the site of the present central library). The Guild Hall is apparently undocumented. Brian has seen no pictures of it and has no date for its construction. Again it was complemented by a lock-up on the other side of the street, built in 1831, although this facility was controlled at different times by the township chief constable or the commissioners for watching, rather than the magistrates, until the Princess St building replaced it. Parts of the lock-up survived into the 1960s, when the area was redeveloped".

The magistrates sat at the Court House in Princess Street, immediately behind the (future) Town Hall. This building was opened in 1847 or 1848, and incorporated a lock-up. It still stands, known now as 'Crown Court Buildings' (presumably reflecting a later change of judicial use) but occupied by the elected Members of Kirklees Council and their immediate support staff".

"From 1881, the magistrates held court in the new court room which was part of the Town Hall. This was linked by a tunnel under Peel Street to the Police Station and the holding cells. The room, now the 'Old Court Room', has been restored in recent years as a public room for hire after a period of use as Council office accommodation".

The premises in Princess Street as seen in 2009 when pictured by the author, all the signs having been removed and the building is now being used for office purposes by the local authority. To the rear the premises are quite extensive.

The Upper Agbrigg Division magistrates held petty sessions in the Princess Street courts every Tuesday, Thursday, and Saturday.

Huddersfield was incorporated as a Borough in 1868 and later in the 19th century borough magistrates were established.

Whether the latter shared accommodation at Princess Street before the Town Hall courtroom opened in 1881 is not quite certain but, from then on until later in the 20th century there was a two court system in the town.

The courtroom could be accessed through a door between the Ramsden Street and Princess Street frontages, and it has now been restored for civic and public function use through that main entrance.

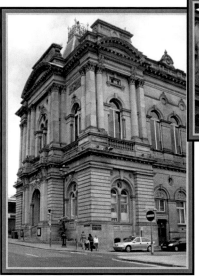

Unfortunately, on the day the author took his pictures, the Town Hall frontage to Ramsden Street was covered in scaffolding but this fine view of the Princess Street end is embellished with a picture of the crest set above the main Ramsden Street entrance.

With the pending local government re-organisation in 1974 when the various boundary reviews took place creating the enlarged entity of Kirklees, the two benches ceased to exist and they merged into one.

Thus in 1973 they joined forces in the new courthouse in its present location, as shown on the following page.

Ted Austen Johnson, a retired Huddersfield magistrate took the trouble to have quite a long talk with the author and he confirmed much of what has been noted above.

He also passed a comment that at one time he thought that magistrates of the West Riding Upper Agbrigg Bench had sat in Slaithwaite, but could not recall where. It may only have been one of these transient affairs brought on by some temporary need, as in many other places, so is not being pursued any further; the observation will suffice.

Somewhat more pictorial in its setting, in this view taken in 2009, the new courthouse building is set adjacent to the Ring Road, and from the front it is architecturally far more pleasing than many others built in the latter part of the 20th century, although the areas to the rear are functional and spacious.

The Huddersfield Magistrates Court opened on 5.2.68
Picture by the author 2009.

The Police Station is backed on to the building, so law and justice in this town are in close proximity to each other.

Holmfirth

The 1845 Petty Session Return for the town refers to the court for the Holmfirth district of the Upper Agbrigg Division being held in the White Hart, Towngate, which was deemed to be a *respectable inn*, in the words of the report.

This picture taken by the author in 2009 shows the White Hart much as it might have been in former years, other than for the modern advertising.

The report also then refers to the fact that a recently built public building had a room to hire for £15 per annum, but it was not thought proper for the clerk to have to pay this out of his modest fee for his services, as there was no public fund available to meet the charge. The clerk, a Mr Martin Kidd of Holmfirth, would no doubt be pleased to have been relieved of this impost.

Matters must have changed in following years as in the 1867/68 West Riding Accounts in Wakefield there is a note to the effect that the courts were held each fortnight in the Town Hall. It is not evident whether the public building referred to in the 1845 return would be the Town Hall or other premises in the town.

However the matter must have been settled at some stage as by the time we get into the second half of the 20th century, Michael Rawnsley, who rose to be Clerk to the Justices in North Yorkshire, recollects as follows .

"I had qualified as a Solicitor by then but still had a period of Articles to fulfil .... so I went to the Huddersfield West Riding Court, clerked by George Nicholson, to finish off my articles for about six

months - he covered Huddersfield WR, Brighouse, Dewsbury WR and Saddleworth. I stayed till Nov 1971 then moved to York".

"Interestingly, the court had a bench that sat at Holmfirth and I can recall going to there on a Friday afternoon with George Nicholson to clerk the courts. He sat in the main hall of the Town Hall and I sat in the kitchen (we cleared the cups and saucers away first - true) I can remember him saying "If you need to get in touch with the office or the Police then use the (public) telephone outside".

The picture above was taken by the author in 2009 and shows that the citizens of Holmfirth were not shy of splashing out funds to show their Victorian success in these fine Town Hall premises. The sub-picture is included for the benefit of many present citizens and visitors to confirm that the building, now known as the Civic Hall, is in fact the former Town Hall.

After the 1974 boundary reviews the West Riding Justices in the Upper Agbrigg Division merged with the Huddersfield Borough magistrates, and all work transferred to court premises in that town.

Uppermill

In the Petty Session returns for 1845, the clerk refers to the court at Uppermill being held in *"a large room occasionally used for public purposes and the Court of Requests"*. It also says *"no rent was charged, the room being the property of the owner of an Inn situate a short distance from it"*.

Various suggestions have been made as to which inn this would be, possibly the Commercial, but so far no firm evidence of that has been found.

So we then move on to later events, and below is the court house which served for much of the 20th century until it was closed.

Uppermill Courthouse.
By courtesy of the Saddleworth Museum Archives – Townswomen's Guild Collection.

Uppermill courthouse was part of the Huddersfield West Riding, Saddleworth, with Michael Rawnsley recalling that .. .

"It was up on the Pennines, no M62, and took me about 2 hours to get there".

He goes on to mention that he recalls the bench sat fortnightly and that one of the staff in charge of the office was called Devy, who was a retired police constable.

The pictures which follow have kindly been provided through the Saddleworth Museum but they are an initiative by the ladies of the Saddleworth Townswomens Guild as part of a photographic project they did recording a year in the life of Saddleworth. They date from 2004; therefore credit and thanks to the Guild are willingly given for their generosity.

Pictures by courtesy of Saddleworth Museum Archives – Townswomen's Guild Collection.

The premises, with the police station next door, were in use at one time as part of the Upper Agbrigg Petty Sessional Division, and apart from any locally residing magistrates any others required would make the journey out from Huddersfield as necessary.

Unless they were already being held in custody by the police any malefactors would progressively appear first in the Court Room (above) and then, if found to be in need of a short period in custody, their route would be via the cell door shown on the right into the custody suite shown below.

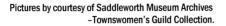

Pictures by courtesy of Saddleworth Museum Archives
-Townswomen's Guild Collection.

This situation continued until the now infamous 1974 local government boundary reviews came about and were implemented, when the district was hi-jacked from Yorkshire to Lancashire.

In due course thereafter the work was transferred down to Oldham or to Huddersfield according to the location of the offence.

Dewsbury

The town did not have its own Petty Sessional Division until that was established in the decade of the 1840s, when it was agreed at the Pontefract Quarter Sessions that the Division be established.

Prior to then, from 1832, there had been a group of townships comprising the Dewsbury Poor Law Union and the justices for that area had sat in the Royal Hotel on Bridge Lane in the town. Francis Ledgard, the Clerk, verified all of this including the fact that the landlord of the Hotel got £10 per annum for the use of the room. In 2009, both the Hotel and the Lane appear to be no longer existent.

In addition there had been a Moot Hall built in 1298 which survived until demolished in the 20th century

Dewsbury Moot Hall
Pictures by courtesy of Kirklees Images Archive.
www.kirkleesimages.org.uk

The 1845 Return of Petty Sessions is unusually verbose in the entry, going on to explain that pursuant to establishment of the new Division the justices were allowed at their own expense to build a court room and offices over the police lock-up and accommodation for the superintendent, which was also authorised to be erected, but the latter were to be a cost to the Riding. Just why the police got their premises free, or at least on the Rates , but the magistrates had to pay for theirs themselves remains a mystery.

The report goes on to say that the scheme had been approved at the Spring Quarter Sessions of the previous year, plans had then been approved by the Secretary of State and that all work was going forward at such a pace that the magistrates would be able to hold the next summer quarter sessions in the new premises.

It is hard to imagine affairs being so promptly completed in today s bureaucratic and administratively complicated procedures.

Remaining with the present day, I am very much indebted to the late Jane Gummer, a long standing friend who served on the bench for many years, for her assistance in tracking down various sources of information as well as providing her own commentary on events within her own time as a justice in Dewsbury.

Her own words are . *"Dewsbury had two courthouses until the 1970s, the town court sat in the Town Hall in a splendid panelled court and the council chamber which was not the most suitable with the largest heaviest chairs in the world! The West Yorkshire Courthouse was for the Spenborough, Heckmondwike and Liversedge areas. We met in Grove Street in a building next door to the old police station. Court No 1 was panelled and splendid with some amazing old paintings of ancient dignitaries on loan from the Saville estates. Court No2 was downstairs without a retiring room, so we sat on the stairs to debate! The courtroom was fully tiled, so it looked a bit like a public lavatory. It had a door through to the adjoining police recreation room, so we could hear them playing snooker in their meal times.*

This building and the police station were pulled down and replaced by the new courthouse in about 1975/6 when the two courts amalgamated and moved together into the new courthouse".

Picture by courtesy of
The Dewsbury Reporter.

The Old Grove Street Police Station and Courthouse.

Such personal references give more of the atmosphere of the times of the late 20th century than many of the more official histories.

The Lost Courthouses of Yorkshire

One can not be other than saddened at the expression *were pulled down* as that has happened to far too many buildings so that our local history has been obliterated other than in the record books. It is the reading of the latter which makes the interested person want to see the structures, but far too many have gone, and the delights of ancient architecture, in physical terms, have been lost for ever.

Dewsbury Town Hall remains a handsome building, and it is shown alongside in this picture taken by the author on a September day in 2009, which shows an ample public space to the front, free from traffic and other encumbrances.

The courthouse which now occupies the old site has its main frontage almost hidden, but the whole utilitarian structure as viewed from Grove Street is shown below.

Convenient and efficient it may be, but it has little to commend it as a work of architectural delight. In 2010 it has been announced that the court is to close.

Pictures by the author
September 2009.

Main front entrance.

Batley

The picture below is of the last Batley courthouse which was situated behind the Town Hall. It was served by two courtrooms and a small office area. Since 1989 the work has moved to Dewsbury.

The Batley Courthouse.
Picture by courtesy of St John Pilkington.

I am extremely obliged to the helpful staff in Batley Library for the following concise information.

Batley became a borough in 1868 by which time it had a police station in Hume Street. In 1877 the town decided to allow the county to continue policing the area rather than setting up its own force and as a result gained its own magistrates court. This venue continued until 1927 when the old police station was replaced.

A court was built, at a cost of £14,000, behind the Town Hall in Brunswick Street. (Batley News article Jan 6th 1927   *New court-house opened at Batley'*.

In the Batley News on Jan 5th 1989 the   *Last court held in Batley'*, was the headline of a further news item.

Wakefield

As with many other places the Manor of Wakefield carried the influence from earlier times and this was geographically extensive, as has been earlier noted, going way over into Calderdale.

Manorial courts would have been held to deal with various administrative and judicial matters. Venues for their sessions would vary. As in other places the justices dealt with a number of matters other than purely judicial, and would have sat where it suited them to do so.

Wakefield had a Toll Booth, in the Market Place which is now called the Bull Ring, but the author is told that this was never used as a courthouse. However, there was a Moot Hall, similarly located, although this was replaced in 1516 with further changes in the 1600s and then managed to survive until 1913 when the last of the Courts Baron was held before it was lost in modernisation of that part of the city centre.

Wakefield Moot Hall, somewhat in a sad state, pictured in 1913 immediately prior to demolition.

Pictures by kind courtesy of the Yorkshire Archaeological Society taken from an album of Pictures of Wakefield on shelf 55M5 pp 32-34.

By 1810 it is known that the justices regularly used the White Hart, opposite the parish church in Kirkgate, holding both petty and quarter sessions therein. This information was provided by John Goodchild to whom I am indebted for his kindness in assisting me.

The White Hart in Kirkgate.
Author's picture

I am very obliged to Kate Taylor, President of the Wakefield Historical Society for providing me with so much information which has enabled me to build up the picture, and any quotations following are from her book *The Making of Wakefield 1801-1900.*

An Act of Parliament of 1795 authorised the construction of a new Sessions or Court House, and a site was selected in Wood Street following a decision by the Reverend William Wood to create the new street. An earlier suggestion to have the building near the House of Correction, now the prison, was abandoned. Various Acts around the time and in the early 1800s brought about the construction of some fine court buildings throughout Yorkshire, Pontefract being one other such place, and Charles Watson the architect expressed his talent in a number of them in a very impressive way.

Wakefield was no exception, and the splendid building is still in place, albeit unused and neglected in 2009. As Kate Taylor notes ..

.... *"It was first used, for the peripatetic Quarter Sessions, on 11 January 1810. According to The Wakefield Star, it had 'glaring defects', 'shew' having been studied more than 'convenience'. The*

91

paper noted that 'The magistrates are comfortably accommodated but the attorneys have scarcely room for more than half of them to sit down. The comfort of the prisoners and their keeper has been carefully consulted but the witness is placed as far as possible from the jury so that his evidence cannot be heard without excessive difficulty'. The Court House was extended in 1849-50".

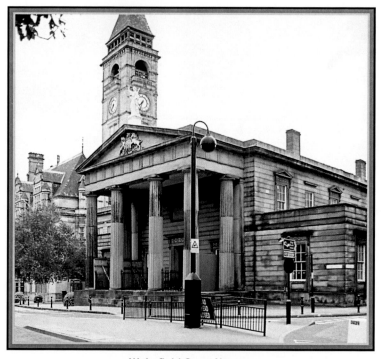

Wakefield Court House.
The clock tower behind is of the Town Hall.
Picture by courtesy of Kate Taylor.

Wakefield was incorporated in 1848, and with that came the desire to have premises worthy of the status of the town. The council met somewhat *ad hoc* in the Court House or in the Public Buildings which had been erected in Wood Street in 1821-3. The committee meetings were generally held in Barstow Square in offices rented from Charles Barstow. Kate Taylor again writes ..

..... *"Councillors would have liked to build a Town Hall but financing it was a daunting problem especially when there was strong opposition by the ratepayers to any 'unnecessary' expense. In 1854, with the intention of providing a Town Hall, the Corporation acquired the 'old croft' a plot of land in Wood Street which had formerly been a quarry, from widow Elizabeth Briggs. Her husband, Isaac, had levelled the land and intended to open a vegetable market there but was prevented under the terms of the Borough Market Company's charter.*

A competition was held for designs, with a £50 prize, which was won by G T Robinson of Leamington. On 21 June the Council determined to seek approval from the General Board of Health to 'mortgage the rates' for the new building. Reaction, when the decision was reported in the local press, was marked. Just as in the past ratepayers had 'requisitioned' the Constable to hold a public meeting, now 1144 of them requested the Mayor to do so.

On 10 July, at the Court House, at a meeting chaired by Edward Sykes (as the Mayor, declaring his support for the scheme, declined to preside), there was a near unanimous vote opposing the Council's decision. The arguments against it ranged from the depressed state of trade, the high taxation because of the war with Russia, the high price of food, the legacy of debt from the Street Commissioners which the ratepayers had to finance, the cost of buying the Manorial Soke rights, which again still had to be met, to the more pressing need for adequate drainage and sewerage and the possibility that the Corporation would buy and extend the water undertaking. Although the Council was anxious to secure an independent Commission of the Peace for the town for which a court-room and offices would be needed, it was argued that it was not necessary to do so".

There were repercussions, as Assizes in the West Riding, which had again arisen as a matter of importance, were in 1864 granted to Leeds, whose fine new Town Hall had been constructed in 1850. It is interesting that although Leeds also had a magnificent Court House that was overlooked for Assize purposes.

Kate Taylor s commentary about the Town Hall and further Court developments is worthy of further quotation ..

"When the Public Buildings in Wood Street came on the market, the Council considered buying that. As late as 1861, still unwilling to commit itself to a new Town Hall, the Council took a ten-year lease of premises in Crown Court which were owned by Jonathan Bayldon and had recently been very substantially damaged by fire, for use as a Council Chamber, committee rooms and offices Its first meeting in the so-called Town Hall was on 9 November 1861".

Wakefield Old Town Hall in 2009.

Picture by the author.

"Wakefield obtained a separate Commission of the Peace in 1870 although for some years prior to that separate Wakefield sessions had been conducted by the Mayor and ex-Mayor under the aegis of the West Riding. The first magistrates were sworn in, eight of them Liberal and four Tory, on 23 March in the small court at the Court House which Wakefield was to use for the next decade. W S Banks, later the author of Walks about Wakefield (1871), was appointed as the first Clerk of the Peace".

"Eventually, in 1875, in a period when the Tories had a majority on the Council, the Corporation bought the Tammy Hall, lying between Back Lane and the George and Crown Yard, and demolished a part of it to allow for a Town Hall to be built on both the Wood Street plot and the newly-cleared site. What was left of the Tammy Hall was converted into premises for Wakefield's police and fire brigade. The architect for the alterations was G H France. A tunnel was begun to allow prisoners to be taken directly to cells in the Town Hall whenever it was built".

"The Wakefield Improvement Act of 1877 authorised the building of the Town Hall. A new competition was held for its design. The scheme of the London-based T E Colcutt was chosen from some thirty schemes, and the Town Hall was built between 1877 and 1880. It had a splendid panelled court room and, immediately below it, three cells from which steps led down to the tunnel".

Wakefield Town Hall.
Picture by the Author 2009.

The Town Hall remained the venue for the Wakefield City magistrates until local government boundary upheavals of 1974 caused the integration with the West Riding justices into one Bench.

On this picture a part of the Court House is to the right.

The Town Hall is to the left of the tower.

It is interesting to read in these extracts how the Wakefield justices first had to share with the use of a minor room in the Court House, before getting their own home in the Town Hall, but in the end, on merging of the Benches, the Court House became redundant.

95

Magistrates who sat in Ossett joined them. Subsequently and nowadays the Bench sits in a courthouse on Cliff Parade. This is in fact the old Police Station which is mentioned as having been linked to the former courts in the Town Hall through a tunnel.

Wakefield Magistrates Courts 2009.
Entrance on Cliff Parade.
Picture by the author.

The view shown does not do justice to the venue.

To the left of the picture is the magnificent, but sadly unused Court House previously shown, and to the right lies the handsome former police station.

The building behind is the side of the Town Hall.

This compact block of buildings is on a site barely 100 yards square, a Victorian feat of civic achievement worthy of the city.

Ossett

By courtesy of the Ossett Historical Society and Ossett Civic Trust, it has been possible to assemble facts which tell us that, following the elevation of Ossett to Borough status in 1890, a Commission of the Peace was granted on 11th December 1893. The first sitting of the new Bench was on 5th March 1894, and that took place in a first floor room in the Mechanics Institute and Technical School on Station Road.

The sketch on the right shows this handsome building in its original form before being converted in to the Borough Library with shops at ground floor level.

Picture by courtesy of
Ossett Historical Society.

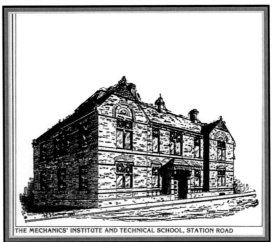

THE MECHANICS' INSTITUTE AND TECHNICAL SCHOOL, STATION ROAD

The history of Ossett Town Hall 1908-2008, compiled by the Ossett Historical Society provides interesting information as follows .. *"The first sitting of the new magistrates was held on Monday morning in the central classroom of the upper floor of the Technical School. A slightly raised platform was arranged for the bench and movable boxes for the witnesses and defendant. The Mayor, Alderman Edward Clay presided There was a crowded attendance of the public and many could not be admitted. The Mayor called upon the magistrates' Clerk, Mr A. M. Lawrence to read Her Majesty's Commission of the Peace.*

The only prisoner brought before the court was Joseph Norcliffe, (52) described as a labourer of no fixed residence who was charged with being drunk and disorderly in the Market Place. The prisoner said he only had two pints between Normanton and Ossett and was on his way to Halifax. The Mayor said that, seeing he was the first case, they would discharge him, but he must try and reform. The discharged prisoner was given a new pair of boots, some clothing, a dinner, and was sent on his way rejoicing".

Such was the relaxed attitude to petty matters in those days.

In 1976 and for some years thereafter, the author recalls in Leeds a charity which dealt similarly with such defendants, but they are now subject to the care of social services.

The magnificent Town Hall only became home to the justices after it was completed in 1908.

Ossett Town Hall.
Picture taken by the author in 2009.

A 2009 official council website promoting the Town Hall as a venue for events says *The Old Court Room offers an atmosphere of intimacy, warmth and timeless understated grandeur.....'*

The *'intimacy and warmth'* can scarcely have been the desire of the Edwardian era justices who set about the business of dealing with local cases after the building was opened in 1908, at a cost of £22,000. To erect this fine building the grammar school was first demolished and moved elsewhere.

Ossett Court Room.
Picture from 'Look back at Ossett, by Norman Ellis, courtesy of Ossett HIstorical Society.

The Borough Court was at the side of the Town Hall.
Down the stairs on the right
is the entry for offenders.
Picture taken by the author 2009.

In 1951, on October 1st, as a result of the 1949 Justice of the Peace Act, the Borough justices ceased to be a separate entity and became a Petty Sessional Division of the West Riding.

Magistrates continued to sit in the Town Hall until the review of boundaries in 1974 when they joined colleagues in Wakefield to be a combined bench. After a little while, justice transferred to that city and has remained there since.

The main furniture of the court was removed to Wakefield, together with many other Town Hall items, including portraits of the former majors of the Borough, most of which have not seen the light of day since then.

Thus demised another proud West Riding Borough, but their spirit lives on and is preserved by a Historical Society and a lively Civic Society. To both of these parties, especially Ruth Nettleton and David Mitchell I am greatly indebted for their assistance.

Pontefract

Eric A Jackson JP has been kind enough to allow the author permission to refer to his excellent work on Pontefract Court House, entitled *Pontefract Sessions House*. The following notes are therefore based on his narrative, but readers who wish to know more should certainly obtain a copy of the original publication.

He remarks that *Whilst the location of the original Saxon Moot Hall, or mound, of Tanshelf, is unknown there was certainly a Moot Hall in Pontefract in 1654'*, but that it lay in ruins, mainly due the sieges of Pontefract Castle during the Civil War. A proposal was put forward that a new Town Hall be built from materials salvaged from the demolished castle.

The present Town Hall dates from 1785 but it is not recorded whether the old materials were used in its construction. Designed by Bernard Hartley to include a court, prison, bank, council chamber, fire station and public hall, as noted on the blue plaque, it was truly a multi-functional building.

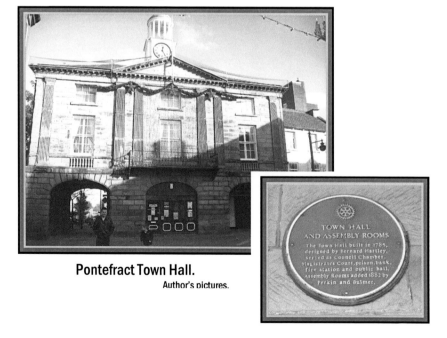

Pontefract Town Hall.

Author's pictures.

Quarter Sessions were held in rotation at various towns throughout the West Riding but as the Easter Sessions were the most important, as the main annual meeting of the justices, these were held at Pontefract in recognition of its historical position as the Riding s largest and most important town during the Middle Ages.

Eric Jackson goes on to say .

"Both the Pontefract and West Riding Quarter Sessions were held in the old Town Hall, which by 1806 had become inadequate, somewhat dilapidated and in urgent need of repair such that in March of that year the Justices made application to: ......

...... "enlarge the existing court house (the Town Hall), the property of Pontefract Borough to make it commodious for the purpose of holding the General Quarter Sessions of the West Riding"; although it would seem that this was never actually done.

As required by the 1806 Act the Justices accordingly gave notice in the **Leeds Mercury** *of 28th March 1807 that application would be made at the Easter Quarter Sessions at Pontefract to both enlarge and alter the existing court house (the Town Hall) and to approve monies out of the rates for a new building including the purchase of land, the notice being signed by Bacon Frank, a Justice of Ferrybridge.*

However, it seems they changed their minds about spending any money on the Town Hall for at the Easter Quarter Sessions they resolved: ".........that the old court house at Pontefract be abandoned and that a new situation be adopted............".

They went on to appoint a committee of Magistrates to carry out this resolution and declared that:

"............the most eligible situation for a new court house is the house and premises late the property of Colonel Ramsden deceased and in so much as a proposition has been made by Mr Taylor of Pontefract, the purchaser respecting the same, that the said committee be instructed to enter into negotiations with the said Mr Taylor on the subject and in the event of their not being able to

make a satisfactory arrangement with him they find some other new situation for the erection of such new court house............ ".

It is uncertain as to when building work actually started at Pontefract, or who the builder was, but the Justices' Account Books show that at the Bradford Sessions on 23rd July 1807 they approved the sum of £2,500 for the new Court House at Pontefract. Over the next five years they approved further annual sums of between £500 and £1,000 towards the building costs, the final £500 being approved at the Wakefield Sessions of Jan 14th 1812, bringing the total expenditure to £6,900, or approximately £400,000 in today's terms.

It seems likely that the court house was finished sometime in late 1812 or early 1813, probably in time for the Easter Quarter Sessions in that year."

Pontefract Court House was designed by Charles Watson, a Wakefield Architect renowned for other notable work in the county.

Main frontage of the Sessions House Pontefract, the current Magistrates Courts. Picture by the author.

The new Court House took all the West Riding justice work from the Town Hall which was left the task of administering civil matters within the town, and as a venue for the borough courts.

The 1845 return of Petty Sessions notes that those for Upper Osgoldcross were held in the West Riding Court House.

Baines in his 1822 work records that the borough justices sat in the Town Hall using the Court Room on the ground floor for the Borough Quarter Sessions, and a Rotation Office which housed *'the magistrates for the town'* on each Monday, when they sat *'for the transaction of magisterial business of the Borough'*. The basement of the premises was a prison. He also notes that the Savings Bank was held there on every Saturday.

Baines then remarks on *'a stately Court House lately built by the Riding; here the principal general Sessions of the Peace for the West Riding of the County of York are held annually in Easter week....'*

Consequently, as with all parts of the country, in the late 20th century the division between borough and county magistrates was eliminated and all cases moved to the Court House. That is the position in the present day, but during the last decade work from Castleford has been transferred to Pontefract and the magistrates for both towns sit in Pontefract.

The rear of the premises also has good architectural merit.
Picture by the author.

In 2010 it has been announced that the court is to close.

Wentbridge

The Return of Petty Sessions in 1845 reports that justices of the Upper Osgoldcross Division sat in a *'room built for the purpose'* in the Bay Horse Inn in Wentbridge, this being considered a place most central in the district.

In 2009, Adrian Judd, the Vicar of Wentbridge advised the author of another likely venue, reputed to be what is now known as Bridge House, with the cottages on the other side of the road having been gaols, with a way under the road by tunnel to the magistrates. Those cottages have recently been refurbished, but a view of them is given below. It transpires Bridge House was the Bay Horse Inn.

The cottages to the left are reputed to have been gaol cells connected to the magistrates premises across the road

Bridge House, the white house to the right, was the Bay Horse Inn in former years.

All the above are now private dwellings.

Author's pictures.

Castleford

Castleford Heritage Trust, especially Mr. Edward Bird, have been most kind in helping to throw some light on judicial matters in that town.

Some notes prepared by Joan Prewer for the West Riding Police Force tell us that prior to 1795 Castleford was such a peaceable place that there was no need for a constable. This changed in that year when the poverty stricken people seized a vessel in the river for its cargo. The military were called in but it does not record what might have happened to the twelve captured offenders.

Before 1857 cases were taken twice a week in the long room of the Ship Inn on Bridge Street and the first prison in the town was just next door. A town lock up was incorporated into Castleford Bridge, repeating a venue in other towns around the county.

In 1862, on the foundation of the West Riding Constabulary, a police station was built in Bradley Street and this provided some accommodation for the magistrates to take cases on two mornings in each week.

This remained in business until 1897-98 when a courthouse and police station were built together on Jessop Street, the road being named after the owner of the land, Dr Adam Jessop. This gentleman was also a magistrate, being the first one appointed for the town, his predecessors in earlier years having been by the authority of the county.

There was a small cell accessed from one courtroom via a staircase, into which all seriously guilty offenders were directed.

Before being turned over to police usage only, the combined building was claimed to be the oldest working combination left in England.

At the time of compiling this piece, the only picture of the No1 courtroom is this modern one taken just before closure. Sadly the fine vaulted ceiling mentioned in earlier times is not to be seen as the all concealing suspended type had taken over.

Castleford No1 Courtroom.
Picture by kind courtesy of Ruth Woodhouse.

Castleford Police Station and Courthouse.
Used until the magistrates moved to Pontefract.
Author's picture taken in 2008.

The departure of the justices was not in one big move, as due to restrictions on space at Pontefract, the Family Court continued to sit at Castleford for some time after the departure of youth and adult to the neighbouring town. It could also accommodate 2-3 day trials if court space was not available at Pontefract or Wakefield.

It seems that regular use for the full range of cases had continued up to the 1990s, this following on from the merger of the Castleford and Pontefract benches in 1974. Some interesting notes have been provided from documents relating to the final closure of the courthouse on 31st March 2005, after consultations had taken place about closure. From 1991 it had been the venue for all Family Court cases for the Pontefract Bench. In addition it was the venue for any lengthy trials which would clutter up the Pontefract premises. In 2002 it was decided that in future all family cases would be heard at Pontefract where suitable accommodation was provided.

The report disclosed that the facilities in the Castleford court premises and for the custody of offenders were not up to required standards and that the cost of improvements, if feasible, would be prohibitive.

The subsequent consultations brought responses from nearly all parties that the premises should be closed, with but one group lamenting the loss of local justice.

Thus the long period of policing and magistrates working together in the one venue ceased. Now, only the police remain.

Aberford and Sherburn in Elmet

Once again we are obliged to the 1845 Return of Petty Sessions for advices that the Lower Skyrack Division sat in a large room at The Rose and Crown Inn on the Aberford main street, which was fitted especially for purpose. The inn was closed some years ago.

The former Rose and Crown Inn at Aberford, now a private residence.

Picture by the author in 2009.

Whilst in Sherburn the Upper Division of Barkston Ash made use of a large room at The Red Bear Inn at Sherburn in Elmet; *'the room with a separate entrance having been provided at the expense of Sir Thomas Gascoigne Bart.,'* the whole business of the division being conducted here.

In 2009 the Red Bear Inn was being totally refurbished, as evidenced in this picture taken by the author in November.

Author's picture.

109

Tadcaster

Tadcaster is a town noted these days on account of the major breweries located there. It was a major staging post on the road to York and would have been such from Roman times. The A64 bypass relieved the town from traffic jams and as with many other country towns it has suffered somewhat with commercial pressure from the big cities, but new investment is providing a firm response.

Baines does not refer to courts in 1822, but the 1845 return of Petty Sessions notes for the West Division of Ainsty these were held in the Bay Horse Inn on the eastern side of the river, that part of the town being in the Ainsty of York. The west side of town was in the wapentake of Barkston Ash, but there is no mention of a court being held on that side of the town. The inn is on the immediate left below.

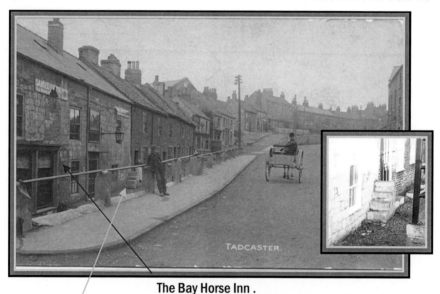

The Bay Horse Inn .
The mounting block shown is in the 2009 picture on the right.
Picture courtesy of Tadcaster Community Archives.

Peter Bradshaw of the local Historical Society has been helpful in finding information about the premises in the town which were used until the Bench merged with Wetherby. He says ....

"The earliest record I have is 1861, Kelly's Trade Directory. The Magistrates' Court was held in the Town Hall which now exists as Sam Smith's Brewery offices, still complete with balcony for making public announcements. The County Courts were held there".

The Old Town Hall.

Pictures by courtesy of Tadcaster Community Archives.

The former Tadcaster Town Hall in 2009.

The picture to the left emphasises the design of the balcony which must have been used in former times to proclaim matters of note in the town.

Author's picture.

Enquiries to a former member of the Brewery management as to whether any of the courtrooms remained identifiable as such in the former Town Hall, produced a negative response.

Peter Bradshaw then follows on by saying

"Following the construction of the Kirkgate Rooms complete with stage in 1880, Petty Sessions were held there from 1889 with the County Court still held in the Town Hall. The Rooms were acquired by the Church in 1904 as a Sunday School but Sessions continued there up to, and I think, until the reorganisation in the 1970s".

**The Kirkgate Rooms,
Built in 1880, housed the magistrates until 1968.**
Picture taken by the author in 2009.

In 1968 the Tadcaster PSD, whose Clerk had been Charles Charlesworth of a Leeds practice with an office in Tadcaster, joined with Wetherby to sit in a new courthouse in the latter town.

In 1974, as a consequence of major local authority boundary reviews, Tadcaster went to North Yorkshire, joining in with Selby in a new PSD which emerged to take in some other areas from around York. Wetherby, which had been moved into the enlarged city of Leeds, then joined the outer Leeds courts.

When originally making enquiries at the local library, one of the staff thought that some courts might have been held in the Council Chamber of the newer Rural District Council offices, but it has not been possible to confirm if that was the case, although from the memory of one lady, the wife of a former magistrate, it is not within her recall, so that seems unlikely.

It is worth dwelling for a moment on Ainsty which was a small wapentake within the area between the rivers Nidd, Ouse and Wharfe, and for an extensive period between 1449 and 1889 was regarded as being attached to York. In that latter year it was made a part of the West Riding, but that changed in 1974 when it was moved to North Yorkshire. Further administrative shuffles in 1996 then split it between York, Harrogate and Selby.

The long period of close links with York is preserved in the name of the York and Ainsty Hunts.

Snaith

Michael Rawnsley, a former Clerk to the Justices in York, has been helpful in providing a great deal of useful information about justice in the county. One of the pieces was that Snaith had its own bench of justices, six of them, which sat in the town.

In past times The Downe Arms in the town had provided the venue for the justices to sit.

In those times, Snaith was a more important town than Goole which only emerged as a major venue with the rise in trade from the West Riding.

Both pictures taken by the author in 2009.

The Courthouse attached to the Police Station was the final venue. In this picture the building to the fore is the old Police Station, the courtroom being the brick building to the rear with the glazed tower providing a source of light.

That came to an end after the 1974 boundary reviews when this small bench joined in with two others from the boundaries of York and with Selby to form the new Selby PSD in North Yorkshire, which then replaced the previous West Riding Selby bench.

THREE
North Yorkshire

One of the first curiosities when discussing the court houses in North Yorkshire is the fact that, under the former disposition of the boundaries within the three Ridings, a number now designated as being in the North lay in the West Riding of the county. Typical of these amongst the larger units were Skipton, Harrogate and Ripon.

It has to be remembered that the North Riding stretched up to Middlesbrough and some other parts of an area familiarly known as Teesside, but did not reach fully to the West of the county. Bearing in mind the width of the county of Yorkshire as a whole, when looking at an old map it is not illogical that the division was aligned to an East and West axis, as the map showed that some of the most northerly areas were also the most westerly, reaching right up into a wedge towards what is now designated as Cumbria.

Apart from main boroughs, such as Richmond, Scarborough, Middlesbrough, and Thornaby on Tees, the remainder of the Riding was divided into urban and rural district councils, in which many market towns were the paramount local units. In some of these there were either courthouses or rooms within the police stations or civic buildings.

A new county borough of Teesside was created in 1968 and this took from the North Riding, Middlesbrough, Redcar, Thornaby and the Eston district with much of Stokesley rural district.

This cosmetic change was short lived as in 1974 the North Riding was abolished.

The county of Cleveland was created, taking in the places mentioned in the preceding paragraph. North Yorkshire was created, retaining the bulk of the North Riding including the districts of Hambleton, Richmondshire, Ryedale and Scarborough, together with parts of the West Riding being added.

The uncomfortable Cleveland county was abolished in 1996, but the name remained in the new Borough of Redcar and Cleveland, which, with Middlesbrough, now lies within the ceremonial county of North Yorkshire. An enlarged Stockton on Tees is partly in North Yorkshire for ceremonial purposes.

Within the present county nomenclature it is probably useful at this stage to mention those which are still open, or are closed. The (W) in brackets indicates those which used to be in the West Riding.

Existing Courthouses (8)	Closed Courthouses (26)
	SEDBERGH (W)
	INGLETON (W)
SKIPTON (W)	SETTLE (W)
	PATELEY BRIDGE (W)
	RIPON (W)
HARROGATE (W)	KNARESBOROUGH(W)
	WATH
	LEYBURN
	BEDALE
	SCORTON
NORTHALLERTON	RICHMOND
	EASINGWOLD
YORK	THIRSK
SELBY (W) *	HELMSLEY
	GRETA BRIDGE
	MALTON, NORTON (2)
	KIRKBY MOORSIDE
SCARBOROUGH	PICKERING
	WHITBY
GUISBOROUGH *	STOKESLEY
MIDDLESBROUGH	SOUTH BANK, THORNABY (2)
	REDCAR, LOFTUS, YARM (3)

*Now in 2011 closed or marked for closure

Other ancient courts such as Aldborough and Tockwith did not continue into later years, and with Boroughbridge are not listed above, although as recorded in the 1845 Petty Sessions Return courts were held in the National School in Boroughbridge into the 19th century.

The West Riding wapentakes have previously been listed and some of these districts lie within the newly devised boundaries of North Yorkshire. On Teeside some cross borough borders, albeit ceremonially, are still linked to North Yorkshire.

The old North Riding of Yorkshire had thirteen wapentakes.

These were named   with sitti   ng benches wholly or mainly at

Allertonshire,	Northallerton
Birdforth,	Thirsk
Bulmer,	Easingwold
Gilling East,	Scorton
Gilling West,	Richmond
Hallikeld,	Wath
Hang East,	Bedale
Hang West,	Leyburn
Langbaurgh East,	Guisborough
Langbaurgh West,	Stokesley
Ryedale,	Norton (Malton)
Pickering Lyth,	Pickering
Whitby Strand,	Whitby

The old Saxon courts, based on these, evolved over several centuries into the local Magistrates Courts as we know them today.

The venues of the court sittings have changed somewhat over the years, as will become evident as the reader follows through the brief stories on the following pages.

York

The history of justice goes well back in the ancient city, and although the Castle is not a normal part of the magistrates domain for sitting it would be wrong not to mention it, as it remains a thousand years old seat for justice in one form or another in the city.

York Castle was originally built in 1068 as a venue to control the North of England by William the Conqueror, who thus continued to emphasise the importance of the city as had been the much earlier Roman custom. Ancient records indicate that the Castle had a gaol, which likely contained as many military prisoners as criminals.

Some two centuries later the castle was rebuilt with the inclusion of Clifford s Tower, and in the 1300s there are records of assizes for the whole of Yorkshire being held in the complex. There are many instances from then onwards where local justices around the county referred serious cases to York Assizes.

Structurally there were several changes in the 18th century. Three new buildings were built adjacent to the Tower. First was the County Gaol, built facing the tower, by William Wakefield in 1701-05. It later also became the Debtors prison.

The County Gaol and Debtors Prison.
Picture taken by the author in 2009.

The provisions on site were further extended later in the same Century with a courthouse and a women s prison, seen below.

A handsome Assize Courts building designed by John Carr was erected to the west of the complex in the period 1773-1777.

The York Courthouse, by John Carr.
Picture taken by the author in 2009.

Nowadays part of the Castle Museum, the female prison was built opposite in the style of John Carr over the period 1780-83.

The Female Prison.
Picture taken by the author in 2009.

There were various other developments in ensuing years, but having been utilised as a military prison at the turn of the 20th century it closed in 1929 when the City Council bought the whole complex.

The central grassed area within the courthouse area is known as Castle Green.

Although some parts of the old Victorian prisons have been demolished the courthouse remains as the York Crown Court, and it receives those cases passed upwards from magistrates jurisdiction.

There are very good detailed works giving a more thorough examination of this complex of buildings on the castle site. This very sketchy *resume* by the author is merely for a little background.

Now let us move back to the magistrates and their venues. Going back to the very earliest days of justice the Archbishop had his own court and at least two gaols, one of these being for ecclesiastical offenders. In addition, the Liberty of St Peter which consisted of the district around the Minster and some places in other parts of York which belonged to it was under the exclusive jurisdiction of the Dean and Chapter, who had their own magistrates, courts and prisons. It had a separate court for the dealing with the other offenders within its jurisdiction. (See ref Baines below) There are mentions of several gaols, kidcotes , or other places of restraint around the city. Many of these appeared to be adjacent to some of the local churches, but it is known that some were near to the Ouse Bridge.

However, this leaves a long gap between those early years where venues changed. Although there was some earlier evidence of premises on the site going back yet another couple of centuries, a Guildhall was built in 1445 which in effect administered the city, in which courts were known to have been taken when it was not in use for other purposes. The trial of Margaret Clitheroe in 1586 was one notable occasion.

The building was built on the site of an earlier common hall which is referred to in the charter of 1256. Local stone was used in its construction and it is known that council meetings were held there in 1459.

Baines, in his 1823 History of York notes that a dungeon was discovered when an inn on the site of the former Chapel of St Sepulchre, near a previous Archbishop s palace to the north of the cathedral , was demolished in 1816. He then tells us that the Hall of

Pleas for the Liberty of St Peter is nearby with a small courtroom on the first floor, going on to explain the extant of the Liberty. He also mentions that the Liberty had its own magistrates and they held quarter sessions at the sessions house in the minster yard.

After a description of the buildings in the Castle area Baines then goes on to list the various Courts of Justice in the city, being the Castle for the County, the Guildhall for the City, and the Liberty of St Peter s, plus an Ecclesiastical Court, in the Minster Yard.

The Return of Petty Sessions in 1845 names the Guildhall as being the place where the magistrates sat, and it seems that this was the main venue for the next half century until the Clifford Street premises were built in 1891 and opened the following year.

The York Guildhall.
Picture taken by the author in 2009,

Some scaffolding is marring the elevation, but in York that can be an occupational hazard when taking pictures.

However, the York Guildhall as it is seen today is largely a reconstruction as an incendiary bomb landed on the hall in April 1942; a direct hit, the premises were reduced to ruin and the stone shell is there to this day (together with the remains of the bomb). It was not until 1956 that reconstruction commenced which culminated in the reopening ceremony by Queen Elizabeth, the Queen Mother, in June 1960.

121

Keith Paver, an archivist in York has been helpful in providing to the author information on the city s heritage in these matters and this is gratefully acknowledged.

Michael Rawnsley, former Clerk to the York Justices and latterly of the Western District of North Yorkshire remarks ...

"York was its own borough and had its own Magistrates court and Quarter Sessions - both courts sat in the Law Courts in Clifford Street (built 1892) until the fusion of Quarter Sessions with Assizes from 1ˢᵗ January 1972 when the Crown Court sat thereafter at the Castle in York and the magistrates were left with exclusive use of the court rooms in Clifford Street".

He continues .. *"Bill Spenceley was Justices Clerk and I was his deputy - the area covered by the PSD was the city area. Bulmer East and Ouse & Derwent PSDs covered peripheral areas - which sat at the Castle and their Justices Clerk was Charles Dixon, a local solicitor who had the part time clerkship. It was Bill Spenceley who told me about a court called York Ainsty which was pre-war and covered the area of York known as Dringhouses but ... that must have been incorporated into York in the 1940s".*

"Nothing changed till 1974 when North Yorkshire was created from the old North Riding, York Borough, bits of the West Riding and bits of the East Riding and possibly bits of Teesside - there were 19 PSDs and nine Justices Clerks, six full time and three part time!"

In the 21ˢᵗ century it is sad to report that this structure has been whittled away to but a handful of courthouses and where the legal framework of Justices Clerks, each supreme in their own right, has diminished to a centrally controlled organisation where the senior legal manager in each location is governed by a county authority.

That body is in turn operating under control of Her Majesty s Courts Service, which is in turn managed by an administration at the behest of politicians and their elasticity of whim according the various crises which strike them, or are generated by the media. The same applies throughout the other Yorkshire counties.

The imposing
and
handsome
Victorian
Magistrates Courts.

The police had premises
in the same building
when it was opened in 1892
on Clifford Street
York.

Picture taken in 2009
by the author.

The panel below is a Dedication of the date of opening, and the main parties concerned with the construction and it is displayed to the right of the building frontage.

Picture taken by the author in 2009.

Selby

The 1974 local authority boundary reviews brought about the move of the Selby township from its position in the West Riding of Yorkshire into the new administrative area of North Yorkshire. What strange thought passed through the minds of the administrators to put a piece of the new county down there is lost with time.

Until then Selby had provided a courthouse for magistrates in that area of the West Riding who were not covered by other major cities or large boroughs.

Richard Moody, a historian in Selby has been kind enough to give of his time to provide some notes of how justice was handled in the town in former years, for which the author is very grateful.

As in other parts, some of the very earliest courts were Leet courts and, in Selby these would likely to be under the control of the Abbots who owned most of the town. As has been mentioned elsewhere the juries of those courts dealt with the management of the Parish and the town as well as matters of law. This is referred to by William Farley, a local historian, in his book published in 1939.

In the period up to 1792 there was a building known as the Middle Row near the Market Cross which extended from the Abbey Great Gateway, immediately opposite the Londesborough Arms. In the rooms above, the Abbots held their courts and in due course the Lords of the Manor did likewise. Sadly, this building suffered the older equivalent of demolition hammers in 1792.

Richard Moody then goes on to quote from Morrell s *History of Selby (1867)* which refers to these buildings as follows ...

"Seventy years ago, prisoners were confined in a cellar forming part of the remains of the monastery adjoining the church, and contiguous to the old Court-house".

A picture from an old print is included on the next page.

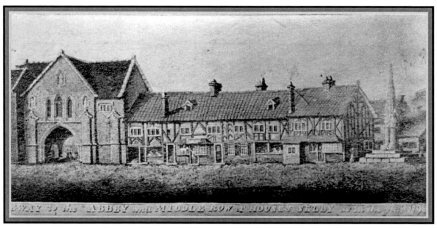

Legend reads: Gateway of Selby Abbey and the Middle Row of houses as in the year 1795.

Picture by courtesy of Richard Moore.

Curley s Trades Directory for Selby in 1960 and 1970 quotes from a source (unknown) .. *"Next to the Market Cross stood the buildings known as Middle Row, extending to the great gateway of the Abbey, over which were the chambers in which the abbots and afterwards the Lords of the Manor held their courts. The gateway, which faced exactly opposite the Londesborough Arms, was pulled down in 1792, and the buildings of Middle Row were demolished 30 years later".*

An item of news amongst the *Pains and Penalties* is notable. In Farley s book there is an item that *"Robert Browne of Cow Lane receives Scotchmen and other suspect people, he is to leave that unruly way, or pay a fine of 40d".*

Worse is to follow because Mr Browne failed to comply with this simple order, it then being recorded under *Offences and Fines* as follows . *"Robert Browne, of Cow Lane, fines 3/4 for receiving Scots and other suspected people".*

Why the Scots should be so singled out in Selby is somewhat of a mystery.

Morrell then goes on to refer to the later changes in premises thus ..

"In 1825, the Town Hall, situate at the corner of Gowthorpe and New-lane, was built, the site being given by the Hon. E. R. Petre. The lower part was intended for cells for prisoners, and the upper room used as a room for the magistrates' meetings."

It is this building which must be referred to in the Return of Petty Sessions for 1845, describing the venue for the courts for this Lower Division of Barkston Ash as being *"A room about 16 feet square over cells used as the lock-up built by subscription in 1826... The room is inconvenient, much too small, and ill adapted for the purposes required* . The Clerk to this affirmation is Thomas Hawden.

Richard Moody and the author have searched for pictures of these premises to no avail. None can be found in the records of the Yorkshire Archaeological Society nor in those of the West Yorkshire Archives at Wakefield. Searches within the town itself including the Library service have proved equally abortive. As Richard said in an email to the author .. *"This loose end will have to remain loose. I have made enquiries, but no one has come up with anything".*

He added that he had been in to Selby Library and looked up what the Selby Times had to say about the Stonelaying Ceremony on July 31st, 1890, for the Town Hall which opened in 1891. Here are some relevant sentences quoting from the Selby Times dated August 1st, 1890 ..

..........*"We know of no town, however unpretentious, which does not possess a building answering to the name of 'Town Hall'. The name is one of dignity, but hitherto the building in Selby conferred no dignity on the town. Those who have been connected with the late Town Hall know it was very inconvenient for holding meetings connected with the town's business, and the Board were unanimous that the time had come for the erection of new buildings".*

The building must have been extremely unloved for it be so disregarded in having it recorded for posterity. However, as often happens in such cases, someone, somewhere may have an image in an old book or file. If that is so, a call to the Courthouse Museum at Ripon would be very welcome.

The new Town Hall, which was erected to replace this one, was never used as a courthouse, so it forms no part of this record.

Mr Hawden continued in office when in 1854 plans were put forward for a new Courthouse and Police Superintendent s house and lock-up in New Lane, which were opened shortly afterwards. James Audus Esq., stumped up the funds to effect the construction, but he had a vested interest in comfort, he being recorded as one of the justices, together with the Revd. Richard Brooke of Gateforth, and Geo Whitehead Esq., of Riccall Hall. Such is recorded by Morrell in his *History of Selby*. That is the situation today, although the Police moved out in the 1980s to a new site in Porthole Road, and the court premises have been re-furbished to modern standards.

With the 1974 changes, a new designated Selby Division was formed, and into this went several components. Tadcaster bench was detached from Wetherby with whom it had only recently been joined in 1968, together with those from Ouse and Derwent divisions and the small bench from Snaith. Together with the domiciled former West Riding Selby justices a new bench was formed which sits in the town courthouse.

These handsome Courthouse premises situated on New Lane were built in the 1850s and included a Superintendent s House and a lock up.

Picture taken by the author in 2009.

The Clerk to the new bench was Bill Spenceley and his deputy was Michael Rawnsley, the latter more recently Clerk to the Justices at York. Interestingly, the latter relates to the author that in the 1970s an effort was made to obtain use of a room in Samuel Smith s offices at Tadcaster. This was presumably because of the 19 mile journey the local magistrates or offenders had to travel without particularly good links between the two towns.

However, the former courtroom in Tadcaster was not made available by the brewery for judicial purposes, so all the business continued to be conducted in Selby, where it remains to this day.

I am greatly obliged to Richard Moody for his kind assistance on the Selby history, and to Michael Rawnsley for his reflections.

In December 2010, despite considerable sums of money being spent in re-furbishing, it has been decided to close the court.

Ewecross Division

The towns which lie in the area which was the West Riding of the county were amongst the parts which were gathered into North Yorkshire in the 1970s, somewhat uncomfortably it may be said. Even some thirty six years later, the affinity of the area still tends to be the route through Skipton and Keighley into the former woollen area of Bradford, as that was how prosperity spread up from the industrial area, as the wealthy sought to escape the smog of the mills.

The late Bryan Braithwaite-Exley JP., DL, a well regarded citizen and magistrate who very kindly corresponded with the author, recalled from his time on the active list . ..

"The Ewecross Division where I first sat was divided into two Benches, one sat in Sedbergh and the other in Ingleton.

We met occasionally together to appoint a Governor to Sedbergh School. We had a purpose built Courthouse in Ingleton. The building was also a Police Station with cells etc.

I cannot remember about Sedbergh, but I think they sat in Sedbergh Rural District Offices.

Settle also had a purpose built Courthouse and Police Station and were East Staincliffe. Ingleton joined them for a short time after 1974 when Sedbergh moved to Kendal. (Note: they went first to Kirkby Lonsdale)

Settle and Ingleton then amalgamated with Skipton Bench (Staincliffe East) in their new Courthouse. No one was very happy.

I do not think that we ever sat in Bentham, and could not say about Grassington".

Some other interesting information about the area is provided by Phil Hudson of Hudson History of Settle who provides an extract from Brayshaws *Giggleswick*.

"By the laws of the 17th and 18th centuries the chief authority in local affairs nominally rested with the justices of the peace, sitting in petty sessions or quarter sessions. But in such self contained

parishes as Giggleswick, where there was seldom a resident justice, the people were, in practice, left to solve their own difficulties. The signatures of two justices were required to give validity to some of their decisions, but this seems to have been a mere formality; and the documents show that the parishioners made and enforced their own bylaws without outside interference.

Their meetings followed the form of the old manor courts, but each township chose its executive officers of the year by vote. The system was in force before the end of the 16th Century, and the officers for Settle, and probably Giggleswick also, were two constables to maintain law and order and arrest criminals, two overseers to take charge of the poor and apprentice their children, and four 'bylawgraves' whose duty it was to see that the manor regulations were respected (especially as regards the common fields of the township), that roads and bridges were maintained in good repair, and nuisances abated. The old Giggleswick bylaws for 1564 and 1603 are still preserved.

Settle probably embarked upon local government at about the same time, but the earliest records that have come down to us only date from the latter half of the 17th Century".

To both of those gentlemen I am grateful for their input and with those preliminary comments, let us move on to examine the individual venues in a little more detail.

Note: Regarding the spelling of Ewcross or Ewecross, this appears to be variable. The old wapentake tends to be referred to as Ewcross, but later interpretations are more noted as Ewecross, especially when referring to the magistrates and associated matters. This book refers to the name just as presented to the author from the various sources.

Sedbergh

Highfield House.

Author's picture.

The fine premises shown above contained the Sedbergh Rural District Council offices and also provided the courtroom to deal with the local cases.

As mentioned by the late Brian Braithwaite-Exley, after the 1974 boundary evolutions, Sedbergh justices moved to Kendal, first via Kirkby Lonsdale.

When Settle and Ingleton later amalgamated with Skipton Bench in the new Skipton Courthouse in 1994 some magistrates who had sat in Sedbergh joined them.

Despite the best efforts of the author, enquiring through a number of contacts, little else has been unearthed on the subject. If any person has knowledge of the times around the late 19th and early 20th centuries, such would be most welcome.

Ingleton

The courthouse at Ingleton, shown overleaf, dates from 1859 when it was first opened and it was built to supersede the previous venue, which was a room in the Wheatsheaf Inn to which access was an external stone staircase. In his book *The History of Ingleton* author John Bentley comments that the justices complained at the blood and entrails of slaughtered sheep which frequently covered the stairs.

I am greatly indebted to John Bentley for his kind cooperation in allowing me access to his publication which enables me to enlarge upon matters of justice in and around Ingleton during earlier years.

As with other places the first stages of justice were the manor courts but, as similarly, the introduction of new parliamentary Acts brought about the establishment of Petty Sessional Divisions in the early to mid nineteenth Century. Coincidentally, under the 1839 Act, the West Riding Police Force was established and they shared the name of Ewecross (that of the old Saxon wapentake) Division with the PSD for the justices. Before then the Wheat Sheaf held sway.

This picture of the Wheat Sheaf Inn taken about 1900 shows the landlord Sam Worthington standing by the front door.

Extract from a picture kindly provided by John Bentley.

John Bentley writes about the Wheat Sheaf, explaining . *"that it is one of the oldest inns in Ingleton .... a blacksmith's shop stood next door, Hodgson's Smithy, which was later added to the inn. The Court House for Ewecross was held in an upper room of the inn, and here the JPs met to renew licences and here all the petty crimes in the villages of the Ewecross Division were dealt with."*

"Not only were Petty Sessions held at the Wheat Sheaf but on many occasions the yearly Court of both the Manor of Twistleton and the Manor of Ingleton were held there, with a sumptuous dinner to follow."

The Licensing and some Coroner s Courts were also held on the premises. That all came to an end in 1859 when the new Court House, custom built for purpose, was opened in the village.

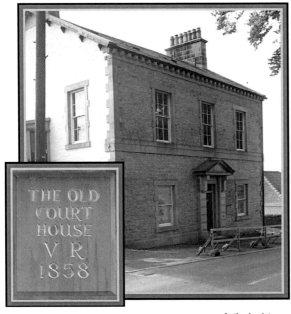

Ingleton Courthouse was built in 1858, but ceased to be used in the latter part of the 20th century when cases were transferred to Settle and ultimately to Skipton.

Author's pictures.

The new courthouse at Ingleton reflected the bipartite nature of the law as by 1860 it also housed the local police Superintendent for the division, as well as having a police office and two cells. Prior to the premises being built prisoners had to be held at the lock-up in Bentham and then brought before the justices at the Wheat Sheaf.

John Bentley astonishingly reveals that the whole project cost £1,000, plus a sum of £75 for the piece of land. When looking at the quality of the premises today one can only marvel at the skill and workmanship available then from a local contractor, Joseph Bentham, for sums of money, which were small even in those days, well before 20th century inflation took hold.

In his description, John Bentley says . *"The court was divided into three compartments. The first was the magistrates' bench room which was 16ft 9in by 12ft 9ins. There was an attached retiring room 12ft 9ins by 8ft. The second part was the court itself measuring 88ft 5ins by 13ft and was provided with table, seats for magistrates, clerk and attorneys. There were witnesses and prisoners boxes and seats with backs for about fifty persons. The third part was an open space for spectators measuring some 35 feet by 12 feet and had a stove for heating".*

His narrative continues . *"Petty Sessions which had been held at the Wheat Sheaf were now held at the new court house. Petty crime was dealt with under the jurisdiction of two of Her Majesty's Justices of the Peace. These JPs came from Ingleton and the surrounding area and made up the Ingleton Bench. None of the JPs distinguished themselves in any way and most were from the local lesser gentry. They were quite severe, arrogant and generally disliked by the local population, yet they kept the legal show running cheaply in Petty Sessions and in Quarter Sessions, which were held four times a year at central places such as Skipton and Wakefield".*

.. continuing with .. *"Brewster Sessions were also held at the courthouse. These were held annually, usually in the first fortnight in February. They met to licence all landlords and deal with inns and ale-houses".*

Further comments reveal that all went sweetly until the 1890s when the position of Ingleton being the place for district justice was tried by a suggestion that the court move to Bentham. It is not really known what had brought on this idea in 1892 but it was rigorously contested by the local inhabitants. A great deal of lobbying went on to stir up protests and a major meeting was held chaired by the local Vicar, the Revd Turner. One aspect of the debate related to whether there needed to be any alterations to the premises, but it was thought that such would be less costly to effect than shifting the whole enterprise to Bentham.

It is not noted how much effort the citizens of Bentham put into lobbying to gain the privilege of having the courthouse but the views of Ingleton residents prevailed and by the turn of the decade and century the long running matter was settled, as Ingleton retained the privilege of having the courthouse.

Now, move on a century when the heavy hand of government and modernisation became the enemy of local justice. The big guns came to bear as consolidation became the issue and the pleas of local opinion came to naught. With the facilities of being able to travel to other towns in a few minutes instead of taking a day or more, and the need to contain costs, the modernisers won the day.

In 1996 the Ingleton courthouse was closed, with the business together with the remnants of Sedbergh bench, which had first been moved to Kirkby Lonsdale and Kendal, descending upon Skipton whence the Settle Bench had two years previously migrated. Thus all magistrates from that part of the former West Riding came together as one body in the new courthouse at Skipton.

Together with the later amalgamations in the adjacent former North Riding area of Leyburn moving over to Northallerton and with Pateley Bridge closing down to Ripon and then to Harrogate, that created a considerable gap in the geography of courthouses in North Yorkshire, bringing to an end several centuries of local justice in a far part of the old West Riding of Yorkshire.

Settle

Phil Hudson, in Settle has been kind enough to provide some background of the likely course of justice and this indicates that before 1600 a Court Barron and Leet were held. These, as noted above, were listed as Giggleswick and were held in various places within the extensive ancient parish.

From 1600 the sequence generally follows the trend as in the other towns within the county, via local inns and the Bishopdale Court House, a name at least 270 years old.

This would have been followed by the Old Toll House in the Market Place which had a lock up and a constable, and later on the Assembly Rooms acted as a court. This was followed by the Town Hall, but possibly not the present one, as by the time that was built the Court House in Station Road was established, and later the premises known as Cragdale House became a combined venue for police and courts.

The Courthouse in Station Road, was up the stairs and set alongside the Police Station, the lock up, and the Inspector s house.

Author's picture.

The former courthouse in Station Road, above, was accessed from an open staircase and is described in a long letter written to the author by Margaret Fazackerley, a reader of the Dalesman now living in Nottingham, who writes

"My family moved there on 1ˢᵗ June1956 from Pudsey, near Leeds. In both cases, my father, Leslie Plumb, was a Police Inspector

in the old West Riding Constabulary. The house at Settle was an old one, attached to the old police station in Station Road which was unused by then, Cragdale House, opposite the end of Station Road, having been taken over as police station, at least on the ground floor. (The upstairs was used by the Health Authority). The new magistrates' court was built on to this building".

Further revelations tell us that .

"The magistrates' bench was at right angles to the sliding door; on going into the courtroom you were looking along the length of the bench from the floor of the court. By 'bench' I mean a raised dais on which the magistrates would sit, behind a continuous leather topped desk like arrangement".

(See the following pages for the entire letter which contains an interesting insight into affairs at that time).

Station Road gave way to premises in a room alongside the Police Station at Cragdale in New Street. This had originally been a trophy room for the owner of the house alongside which served as the police station, which it still did in 2008.

Court sittings continued to be held there until 1994 when the seat of justice was shifted to Skipton.

This was the entrance to the court in what was previously Cragdale on New Street.

It closed when the justices transferred to Skipton.

Author's picture.

137

APPENDIX re SETTLE.

Letter from Margaret Fazackerley to the author about Settle Court House and related matters.

As promised, some "bits and pieces" about living at the old Court House in Settle.

My family moved there on 1ˢᵗ June 1956, from Pudsey, near Leeds. In both places, my father, Leslie Plumb, was a Police Inspector in the old West Riding Constabulary. The house at Settle was an old one, attached to the old police station in Station Road. The old police station was unused by then, Cragdale House, opposite the end of Station Road, having being taken over as police station, at least on the ground floor. (The upstairs was used by the Health Authority.) The new magistrates' court was built on to this building.

Although the old station was unused, it must have still "belonged" to the police force, because, as I have said, we lived in the attached house, and the upstairs of the old station had been turned into a flat, occupied when we moved in by a Mr Mackley, a police constable, and his wife. Later the flat was occupied by PC Light, and his wife and baby. Our house had four bedrooms but the one I occupied was at the end of the corridor upstairs and up a step, and was in fact over the old police station below. At some point in the past this room must have been created by pinching a room from the upstairs of the police station, to create another bedroom. There were some cells in the old station, and very occasionally these were occupied overnight, presumably when there was an overflow in the new police station. I can remember once or twice being told by my mother not to be alarmed if I heard voices downstairs in the night - it was only prisoners in the cells.

There was a courtyard at the side of our house, separating it from the old court house. At the back of the yard, a very high wall screened us from the grounds of the Ashfield Hotel (now a Trade Union headquarters, I think.) In our time, there was a pair of large solid wooden gates screening the yard from the street, so we were completely private. The yard was flagged with large stone slabs, which tended to be slippery when wet. Opposite our front door, across the yard, were two or three steps up to a door which had two patterned glass panels. This door led to a sharp left turn up a steep narrow staircase. At the top were two doors; one leading straight on, up another step, into an anteroom, the other a sliding door on the right which opened directly into the court room. The partitioning surrounding this staircase at the top was glass-panelled. This whole building "went" with our house, and was regarded as our private playground. ("Our" being myself and brothers aged 5 or 6, and 12.)

The magistrates' bench itself was at right angles to the sliding door; on going into the courtroom you were looking along the length of the bench, from the floor of the court. By "bench" I mean a raised dais, on which the magistrates would sit, behind a continuous leather-topped desk-like arrangement. I seem to think there were inkwells at intervals, but I couldn't swear to this. On the public side of the bench was a low seat running its length. I imagine the clerks etc would sit here, facing the courtroom. The bench ran most of the way across the room, but stopped a few feet short, to allow access to the witness room (see below).

The public entrance to this building was up a long outside stone staircase, parallel to, and leading up from, the street below, and consisted of large double doors, always firmly locked and bolted during my time. The courtroom was large, painted in a light colour, with flooring of some kind of lino. Windows were either dingy or frosted glass, I can't remember which, but possibly both. The woodwork was a kind of ginger colour, and treated to look like wood graining, although this was done with paint. In one corner, by the end of the bench, was a door which was padded on the inside with green baize, presumably to sound-proof it. The door led into a small room which I assume was a waiting room for witnesses. This room was at the same end of the court as the anteroom mentioned above, and was next to it; however, the door to the "witness" room led directly from the court room, across the end of the bench, whereas the anteroom could be accessed only from the staircase, or the bench itself.

The anteroom had an antique-looking washbasin, and a built-in cupboard of some sort. The only toilet was down the staircase to the courtyard, turn sharp right through an archway in the downstairs wall of the court house, and left into a lavatory, very cold and dark. In the court room itself, and a source of hours of entertainment for my brothers and myself, was the movable courtroom furniture: several strong wooden benches, the kind well-reinforced underneath with a plank running their length; the jury box; the witness box. These were all self-contained, and would slide about quite easily on the linoleum floor. I can't imagine why they didn't go to the new courtroom; presumably it was kitted out with new furniture. Whatever the reason, we were able to use them to build space ships, fortresses and so on; you can imagine!

They were all the same ginger colour as before. We spent hours and hours playing in there, during the winter at least; incidentally, there was never any heating; I don't remember there being any radiators, and if there were I can't imagine where the boiler would have been. We built a museum in the anteroom once, displaying plastic dinosaurs from cornflake packets, and I remember subjecting my poor mother to a terrible concert, put on by me and some friends.

That pretty well describes the inside of the courtroom. Downstairs in the courtyard, on the right as you came in from the street, before the back door to the court was reached, was a stable door, the usual type divided into two, leading into a cobbled stable which was under the courtroom. This still had a metal manger fastened to the wall. I assume that the Police Inspector still got about on horseback when the building was erected. My brother fixed a strong loop of rope in the doorway, door open of course, and with a carefully placed cushion I had a kind of swing which kept me happy for ages.

After the stable door was the courtroom back entrance described earlier, then the archway leading to the lavatory. Also through the archway was a shady unlit area housing our dustbins. At the end of the yard on the right, still part of the court building, was a wash-house, unused by us. It had a stone sink and I think was tiled with glazed bricks. These areas were unlit and cobwebby.

Right at the other end of the old police station building was a double gateway into another yard. At the opposite side of the yard to the police station was another old stable building, made into a garage where my father kept his car. The upstairs of this housed a full-sized billiard table which off-duty policemen used sometimes. In one corner of the yard was an incredibly ancient petrol pump, long disused, which apparently was used for police cars at one time. In this corner of the yard was a doorway to a very long narrow yard which went round the back of the police station and house, to a back door of our house. This yard was known as the "dog yard", although I never saw any dogs there! I have though seen an old photo in a book about the history of Settle, showing "otter hounds" in Station Street, in front of the old police station. Whose they were, and where the otters might have been that they hunted, if they did, I can't imagine!

These are turning into rather long "bits and pieces", but having started, I'll finish!

The Lost Courthouses of Yorkshire

I was surprised to find, when we moved to Settle, that the Police Inspector was (relatively speaking, of course - this was 1956) a Somebody; a big fish in a small pond, I suppose. I used to read the local paper, the Craven Herald, I think, and would regularly see my father's name in the court reports, something on the lines of Inspector L. Plumb (pros.) said.... "I'm not very familiar with how magistrates courts work nowadays, but surely police use solicitors to bring prosecutions, rather than doing everything themselves, don't they? I remember my father being called upon to help organise a new youth club. His "patch" was enormous, and included Sedbergh and Dent, now in Cumbria.

As I said earlier, Cragdale House, then as now, was the police station. The front door always stood open, and immediately on the left of the door inside used to be a set of stocks, now housed in the local museum, I think. There was a staircase up at the back of the hall to the health authority; I sometimes had to hand-deliver letters there from the headmaster at the junior school where I was a pupil. On the left downstairs was a door into a busy office, housing clerical staff and any policemen who happened to be around. On the right was a door to a corridor, and leading off this also on the right was my father's office, just as big as the other one, but practically empty apart from a filing cabinet or two, and his enormous roll-top desk. I had strict orders from my mother that I must never go into this room without first checking with the main office that he was alone.

My mother told me years later that during our time at Settle, a cache of wine was discovered somewhere in Cragdale House; I have an idea it had been walled-up somewhere, perhaps for safe keeping in a cellar during the war. Anyway, my father, conscientious as ever, carefully recorded every bottle and handed it all over to The Authorities (not sure who this was); he didn't bring even one bottle home, and she never quite forgave him!

Settle being in the middle of a caving and potholing area, the local Cave Rescue Organisation was centred and co-ordinated on Settle police station. When there was an emergency, in those pre-mobile phone days, the big tree in front of Cragdale used to have a big canvas banner tied round the trunk, reading "Cave Rescue Out" so as to attract the attention of any passing members.

We lived at Settle for four years, some of the happiest of my life. I've visited occasionally since. In 1984, 1 think it was, the old Court House was evidently being used as a base and rehearsal room for the local Light Operatic Society. ..The outside staircase from Station Road had a large notice at the top, saying it was the "home of Settle Operatic Society" (or whatever the exact title was). On later visits, the notice had gone.

On the same visit, the old stable was in use as a gift shop selling souvenir-type things like pot pourri and candles. The big gates had gone; I seem to recall there were still gates (wrought iron, I think?) but set further back. I ventured up to the house; it had been taken over as an accountant's office, and the owner very kindly allowed me to have a look inside. It was much altered; walls removed, the front door bricked up, etc. At the far end of the building, where the yard with the petrol pump used to be, was now a new road from Station Road to Kirkgate, cutting through the old Ashfield Hotel grounds; the old garage was gone.

The last time I visited Settle, the gates to the yard had gone altogether, and I once again visited the house; the same accountant was still there, and again kindly allowed me to look inside. It was startling to see a spiral staircase ascending into what had once been my bedroom! The souvenir shop had closed, and there was no clue as to what use, if any, was being made of the old Court House - but it was still there.

*Sorry this has turned out to be so lengthy, and probably largely irrelevant, but I hope there may be something you can use. I've just re-read the original query in your email, and realise I may have misinterpreted your query. Were you asking if the police station and court all moved at the same time from Station Road to Cragdale, or did one or the other go first? If this is what you mean, then I have to say, I don't know; **I only know that neither of the old buildings was in use by 1956.***

I hope this helps a bit. With all good wishes

Yours sincerely,

Margaret Fazackerley

Skipton

In 1845, the Return of Petty Sessions states that these were held in the Town Hall, then in the ownership of the Earl of Thanet, a room being provided free of charge for that purpose. The Clerk who submitted this return was Richard Greenwood of Gargrave and the sittings were of the Skipton Division of Staincliffe East. Of interest is a note that in Gargrave, for Staincliffe East, sessions were held in the private office of Mr Samuel Hall.

However, the building which is known today in Skipton as the Town Hall was not the one in use at the time. That building is at the upper end of a wide area below the church which is not unreasonably called Church Street.

Towards the lower end it divides into two parts, the section to the East side being named Market Place and the opposite narrower portion being named Sheep Street. In between is a line of buildings collectively known as Middle Row, and in the centre of the Row is the Old Town Hall. This is the building to which reference is made in the Return and to which Baines also refers in his 1822 discourse on the county.

The Market Place elevation of the old Town Hall is shown on the left.

Author's pictures.

The plaque to the right is set on an adjacent bank and notes the presence of a law enforcing item.

IMMEDIATELY IN FRONT OF THIS BANK STOOD THE PILLORY WHICH WAS TAKEN DOWN A.D. 1770; ALSO THE MARKET CROSS AND STOCKS WHICH WERE REMOVED A.D. 1840.

However, the best view of the old Town Hall is from Sheep Street, on the left, to either side of the stone steps there being the stocks as used in those times.

Reproduced with kind permission of North Yorkshire County Council and Mrs V Rowley.

The imposing premises higher up Church Street were built for public entertainment in 1862, and it was not until 1895, when Skipton Urban District Council was created, that the hall was bought from its private owners, enlarged and turned to more formal use as the Town Hall with a Council Chamber and sometimes for the courts for some sessions. The Sheep Street Town Hall ceased to be used.

This view shows the 19th C Town Hall and the adjacent Council offices.

Reproduced with kind permission of North Yorkshire County Council and Mrs V Rowley.

A new courthouse was then provided on Otley Street and this continued to hold the sittings for magistrates until 1973.

The building as shown alongside is now labelled as The Old Courthouse, but happily it is well preserved as a fine comparison against its modern successor on the same street.

Picture taken by the author in 2009

The modern Skipton Courthouse
Picture taken by the author in 2009

The building shown above now serves the magistrates and the County Court, the latter sessions being held on two days when the magistrates are not taking their cases. In addition the court offices are contained therein, having moved from the Ship Building in Caroline Square in the year of opening, 1973.

In due course all business from the courts previously further up the old West Riding, gradually came down to Skipton.

Thus, the whole area which had stretched in the West Riding from Skipton to the most far north westerly point of the junction of the old county with Lancashire and what is now called Cumbria, has its local justice enforcement taken miles away from the towns and villages which still form the communities which might have been so offended by crime.

The next nearest courthouse these days in North Yorkshire is at Harrogate, all of the others in the area having been closed. Further away availability is at Northallerton.

The 2010 review which was undertaken by HMCTS seemed to concentrate on the simple distances between the open and closed courthouses, not for the hinterland for which they are responsible. Thus their suggested simple journeys bear little relation to the facts in many instances. As has been shown and demonstrated by the local MP, the journey from Bentham to Skipton is straight forward, but from the former town to Harrogate is more complex and very lengthy.

Sense has prevailed and Skipton will continue to serve people as a seat of magisterial justice.

I am also grateful to Sue Wrathmell, involved with the Skipton Community Research Project, for her useful input to my researches.

Kildwick

There is mention of a Justice Room at Kildwick Hall, between Skipton and Keighley, with various pictures being shown of a rather neat building which has much of the appearance of such a venue in those earlier times.

However, no evidence has been presented or provided to the author that this building ever served such a purpose, and it can only be assumed that it acquired that name by its looks but not by any use for the purpose.

In the absence of further alternative information the premises will not feature on these pages.

Pateley Bridge

As was the case with many other towns, there was a Manorial Court in the Middle Ages in Pateley Bridge and this dealt with such as property transfers and other town managerial matters. All criminal cases were normally sent to Ripon.

43 High Street.
Picture by the author.

In the 19th century the local court was held at premises on 43 High Street and was still there in 1880.

Some time in the 1840s the magistrates at Pateley who had been sitting as part of the Liberty division removed themselves from the courthouse at Ripon and decided to sit at Pateley, despite there being concerns at the accessibility of the place for those destined to be brought before them.

However, as there is no return of Petty Sessions for the town in 1845, the move was probably not until later in the decade.

This debate rumbled on until 1862 when they eventually appointed a Clerk, Mr Sykes on a part time basis, who was employed in another job at the local lead mines office.

He served a new combination of Nidderdale justices which had arisen as a result of the 1820s Parliamentary legislation, but they were still, at times, being assisted by Ripon colleagues who journeyed to the town. They sat at 43 High Street.

147

The Police Station was built in 1897 and a specific courthouse was sought and it was only in 1902 that premises were opened in Church Street, although there appears to be a difference in dates according to various sources. It is noted that the furniture for the courthouse was specially made by Marsh, Jones and Cribb of Leeds.

Pateley Bridge Courthouse with commemorative plaque.

Pictures taken by the author in 2009.

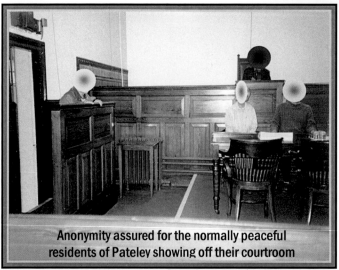

Anonymity assured for the normally peaceful residents of Pateley showing off their courtroom

Picture by courtesy of the Nidderdale Museum.

Despite some possible change in 1955, which came to naught, this venue remained as the Pateley Courthouse until 1993 when the division was once again amalgamated with Ripon, the premises at Pateley later being closed.

Built in 1897, closed in 1995 says the plaque, the premises are now converted into apartments. The front portion shown is about the only part resembling the original building.

The matter of dates relating to events is one which has caused the author much concern throughout this book. Authorities produce varying dates. This is an example where information from one source to the author is different to the date given on the plaque. There is a suggestion that although the courts closed for regular business at the earlier date there was irregular usage up until final closure.

Ripon

Anthony Chadwick, a former Ripon magistrate, who with others is responsible for the Ripon Courthouse Museum and its care, has been kind enough to provide some useful information about the work on law and order in the city.

I am obliged to him for some explanation of the circumstances in that ancient city in answer to my request, and I quote

You have hit upon a matter which has foxed most people who try to understand this matter, so I'm afraid that the explanation is a little involved.

After the Conquest the Archbishop divided his manor to create a manor for the minster prebendaries. The two manorial courts were two buildings, with the canons' court being to the west, and the predecessor to the Georgian building to the east. From the 14th Century the Liberty Court became also a Quarter Sessions courthouse. This courthouse was rebuilt in 1830.

Under the canon's court was a dungeon used for debtors. But Howard (of the Howard league) came to Ripon and condemned the dungeon. It was filled in and the whole building made in to the gaol, with the keeper's house to the south where the exposed timbers can be seen.

Meanwhile the Liberty Court had created a House of Correction for criminals, and the canons met in a room there, thereafter.

The gaol was abandoned in the late 19th Century, and the building has since been a souvenir shop and private house".

On the following pages are pictures of some of the buildings which are referred to in that narrative, and it is to the credit of the City, the Church and the Museum authorities that such care has been taken to preserve these historic premises.

The former Canon's court entrance above with, below, a sighting of the former court house as it is seen over the top of the wall.
Author's pictures.

This rather nice compact building housed the Ripon Liberty bench until 1998, when it closed and the work was transferred to Harrogate together with the cases from the former Pateley Bridge courthouse which had joined it at Ripon several years previously.

The plaque reads 'From Anglo Saxon times until 1888, Ripon had its own independent system for maintaining law & order, the Ripon Liberty. Its courthouse stood on this site, within the Archbishop of York's summer palace. This was replaced in 1830 by the present building which housed the Quarter and Petty Sessions and later the magistrates' court. After this closed in 1998 the original building became a museum.

Author's pictures.

The pictures on the next page are of scenes staged within the museum itself, showing typical views of participants on both sides of the bench.

The upper one is seen across the bench, whilst the one beneath illustrates how those appearing would be seen on entering the court room. The severe looking chap in front is the Justices Clerk.

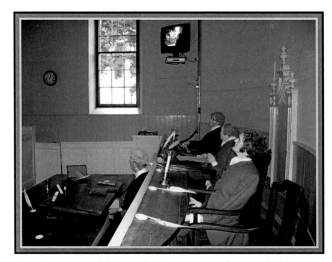

This picture which shows 3 dummy justices in session was taken from the point where the magistrates entered to take their places.

The entire room is only about 35 square, so the justices would be within range of any violent or excited customer .

Author's pictures.

All the Pictures of the Ripon Courthouse
are taken by courtesy of the Ripon Museum Trust.

153

Knaresborough

From Norman times there were three areas in and around the town, The Forest of Knaresborough, The Borough (the town), and the Forest Liberty. Each of these had its own court and constable. In the 13th century the Archbishop of York established a Prebend of Beechall thus adding another court sitting once a year.

By the mid 15th century there were the Forest Liberty courts being held in the Old Courthouse in the castle grounds and the Borough court in the old Toll Booth in the Market Place, the latter being taken by a Borough Bailiff on a fortnightly basis.

Author's pictures in 2009.

The building in the grounds of the Castle is noted as the Courthouse and Prison for the Liberty of the Forest of Knaresborough.

Petty-sessions were held before the steward (a barrister) and under-steward of the Duchy of Lancaster.

This was the oldest court building in Knaresborough, dating from the Tudor period, with parts from before then and some later additions in the 18th and 19th centuries; but there were also the borough courts held in the town as noted above, and others for the West Riding in a separate courthouse which was built in 1838. This also housed the police.

Knaresborough itself was the centre for legal jurisdiction in these parts, and as will be noted from the entry for Harrogate, that later Spa town only received its own authority to hold courts very late in the 19th century. Prior to then Knaresborough and the Duchy of Lancaster ruled the roost in all matters relating to law and justice. The lessee of the Manor was the Duke of Devonshire.

By the mid 18th century the Borough Court building and Session House in the old Toll Booth was being rebuilt as the Town Hall, with the addition of cells beneath, the latter being subject of much criticism by Howard, the prison reformer, on account of their condition.

In 2009 The Old Town Hall built in 1862 in the market place on the site where the former Toll Booth was situated.

It is a dignified reminder of a very fine venue of former years, albeit now given over to being a shopping centre on the ground floor.

Author's picture.

The Parliamentary Return of Sessions for 1845 is couched in the following terms *"...The room in which the justices transact the business of petty sessions for the Wapentake of Claro, during the six months of winter, is 19 feet two inches in length, and 16 feet 9 inches in breadth, which they are obliged to use for the advantage of fireplace thereto; it forms part of the Sessions House. For the remaining six months the petty sessions are held in the Court House in which the quarter sessions for the West Riding are held".*

Magistrates sitting in some courts in the 20th century would have been grateful for that amount of consideration.

The Court House to which the latter West Riding reference is made would be the one built in 1838 shown alongside which, it is reported, cost the rather modest sum of £2,000.

In 1968 that building was demolished and it seems that the courts then transferred the sittings to the premises shown below, barely 100 yards away.

Knaresborough Police Station and Courthouse.
Sketch by R A Curry from an old print.

The Urban District Council premises.
Author's picture.

Tom Bolton certainly recalls that the magistrates held court in the former Urban District Council offices, built in 1910, seen above, at the corner of York Place and Gracious Street, and it is clearly marked on the Ordnance Survey of the town at the time as Court House. The

Castlegate site of the old courthouse and police station then became the place for redevelopment with the new buildings as seen below.

This is the police station. The magistrates sat in a room provided, but there was not any place for the officers who had to make do with a loan of offices from a local solicitor on the nearby High Street.

1960s Police Station.
Picture by the author.

It is difficult to see how planning authorities could permit such a misfit to be erected adjacent to the historic castle yard.

Ken Harding, a Justices Clerk who came to Knaresborough in 1971 mentions that the magistrates were sitting in this police station when he arrived, but that ceased in 1974 when boundary changes did away with the separate boroughs of Knaresborough and Harrogate and they became one PSD. Shortly afterwards, the justices transferred to Raglan Street in Harrogate but the police remained in Knaresborough.

The imposing former council offices cum temporary court building on Gracious Street is no longer in use for council or justice purposes and is occupied by general offices.

Knaresborough with all its ancient court history and former eminence over its younger neighbour, Harrogate, no longer dispenses justice within its own boundaries. Centuries of judicial activity were reduced to notes in old records at the stroke of a parliamentary pen which enabled the final Act.

Harrogate

Despite its present day importance, Harrogate in very early times was a mere adjunct of greater places like Knaresborough, and its record of magistracy is only from later in the 19th century. Whereas its now lesser neighbour, Knaresborough, had the title of the ancient Forest of that name, and such matters as justice were very much controlled by that town.

Malcolm Neesam, the celebrated Harrogate historian wrote to the author, ...

"For centuries, Harrogate affairs were looked after by the Royal Court of the Honour of Knaresborough, administered by the Duchy of Lancaster".......

......"One of the main reasons for Harrogate obtaining the 1884 Charter of Incorporation was that the town would have its own Courthouse. Shortly after 1884 a gothic-styled villa was acquired in Raglan Street, and this occupied the Borough Court for about twenty years, until it was replaced......... by the building now occupied by Stowes Solicitors. The police worked from a house in Raglan Street; ......".

Early Harrogate had relied on a historical tradition of policing which was by Township Constables from such as Pannal Township, and others. Knaresborough was still the centre for all appointments and magistracy. As Harrogate developed it was allowed a policeman of its own who was formally appointed by and subject to the Knaresborough Court. This remained the case until the West Riding Constabulary was formed in January 1857.

For those with an interest in the police, there is an excellent book by Clarrie East entitled *The Constables of Claro* and this gentleman has also been of great help to the author in his researches around Harrogate and Knaresborough. In this he points out that the early constables occasionally attended court hearings at local inns, although the main venue for such was Knaresborough. Two such places were the Bay Horse, later the Empress Hotel, and Hattersleys

Inn, long since overtaken by the Prince of Wales Hotel and now apartments.

Grainge in his 1871 publication of *Harrogate and the Forest of Knaresborough,* on page 194 refers to *"......on the right is Raglan Street, in which is situate the Police Station, a neat brick building, erected in 1866".*

Police outside the former 'red brick' police station in Raglan Street.
Picture by courtesy of Malcom Neesam.

In 1881 Harrogate formerly asked Knaresborough for its own court. This was rejected by Knaresborough and they suggested that Harrogate should apply for two more county magistrates to make a total of six and that Harrogate should approach county magistrates to see whether a day could be fixed for transacting business in the town.

Harrogate suggested also that part of the police station could be used for occasional petty sessional courts, although these would still form part of the Knaresborough jurisdiction.

Harrogate was incorporated as a Borough in 1884 and from then it seems that the town was allowed to have its own independent justices. (Details from History of Harrogate under the Improvement Commissioners 1841 1884; H H Walker).

The first court building was in Raglan Street, and an old negative has provided the following print, by courtesy of Malcolm

Neesam. This plainly is the same building as the police station noted above. The bay window and front door are a clear match.

The old Raglan St building, taken at the time of its demise. Removed window frames are shown leaning on the railings.

Picture by courtesy of Malcolm Neesam.

As remarked upon by Malcolm Neesam, it seems that this converted villa served the purpose of courthouse until some time in the last decade of the 19th century, when it was replaced by the building which remains on the site. It is not certain where the courts were held during the re-construction, but Malcolm Neesam suggests possibly in the Victoria Baths building which was converted later in the 20th century into the council offices of today.

The new courthouse had substantial cells and the police shared the accommodation until 1930 when a new Police Station was built in North Park Road. However an Inspector continued to live in the attached house on Raglan Street for some years thereafter. John Moore of Stowes Solicitors, who has been searching details wrote ..

"I understand from one of my colleagues, that he believes the building was constructed in the late 1890s and was originally a Police Station. It then later became a Court House. Following its use as a Court House it was then used to house refugees in the Kosovan conflict prior to our use of the building by Solicitors".

160

There were some curious features in those premises, such as the custody facilities for some defendants who had to wait their turn in far from ideal circumstances, bringing once more into play the theme of half way down the stairs . As Tom Bolton, a retired magistrate recalls; *"The flight of stairs* (on the right hand of the building when viewed from the front) *leading to the court was provided with flap down seats on which the posteriors of 'customers' were rested whilst awaiting their appearance".*

The former Raglan Street Courthouse.

Author's picture.

The Old Court House in Raglan Street is now the principal office of Stowe Family Law LLP, of which Marilyn Stowe is the senior partner. She says .. *"We have been practicing here since April 2004 before which the building was empty for some years after its conversion to offices. **The basement used to be the cells and my room is where the solicitors used to wait before going into court, which now is the home of a number of secretaries!** I remember appearing here in the days when I used to go the Magistrates Court – a long time ago. I started from very humble beginnings in Halton, East Leeds, in a converted cobblers shop with three clients, a secretary and a second mortgage to fund it(!) and now head up a*

161

family law practice in North Yorkshire and Cheshire, ... enhanced by the beautiful building from which we are so fortunate to work".

How nice that a building used for so long in the workings of justice has now just not become another themed public house.

However, Raglan Street was not blessed with all the modern facilities. By the latter part of the 20th century it became necessary to have more commodious premises, which would also take the courts decreed by Government to be merged with the Harrogate Bench.

Illustrated below is the present courthouse on Victoria Avenue in Harrogate. Custom built to the very latest Home Office needs it was opened March 1991, the magistrates sitting from April. Situated but a long stones throw from its predecessor it has brought together the magistrates from the Ripon Liberty and Claro divisions, situated in Nidderdale and to the North of the spa town, of course including the ancient courts of Knaresborough.

The Magistrates Courthouse on Victoria Avenue now houses Harrogate, Ripon, Knaresborough and Pateley Bridge courts.

Author's picture.

Wath

In the course of the narrative about each location references may have been made to older buildings where some courts were held, not always in premises officially designated as a court house , these at some times merely being a *pied a terre* for the purpose of justice being dispensed.

One example of this situation lay with the Halikeld justices who for many years sat at York Gate Farmhouse which now remains no more than a ruin at Baldersby on the west side of the A1, but by the mid part of the 20th century they had moved to a room above the police station at Wath, as shown below.

Wath Police Station and Courthouse.
Picture by courtesy of Paul Sherwood.

That courthouse closed in the 1970s and the bench first moved to Ripon, a move much disliked because Ripon was still in the West Riding, but it then moved to Thirsk, before finally being merged in with Northallerton in 1996.

Leyburn

In his 1823 treatise Baines is silent in the matter of justice. However, the petty sessions return for 1845 records the use of a room at the Bolton Arms as the venue for justices of the Hang West bench.

Bolton Arms, Leyburn.
Picture courtesy of Paul Sherwood.

Later, the Leyburn court was basically held in a room on the first floor of the Town Hall, which had been built in 1857.

Leyburn Town Hall .
Picture by courtesy of Paul Sherwood.

However, the justices moved from there to sit at the nearby Thornborough Hall in Leyburn.

Thornborough Hall, Leyburn.
Picture by courtesy of Paul Sherwood.

It was at times necessary to have additional courts and these could have been held at the police station in Leyburn, or at times in Hawes further up Wensleydale.

The latter occasions would probably mainly have been when inclement weather prevented the justices from making the journey to Leyburn and used the local inn.

The magistrates continued to sit in Thornborough Hall before moving to Richmond in 1996.

Muker

Like Aldborough and Tockwith, this is more of a historical matter rather than the loss of a 19th century custom built courthouse as the result of reductions and reorganisations within the court service in the 20th century.

Muker, lying in Swaledale, these days is a small and fairly quiet place but that was not always so as during the 18th and early 19th centuries it was a centre for much of the mineral mining which took place in the Dales, the population being quoted by Baines as 1,425 inhabitants in 1823. By nature of the rough and hazardous occupations and the people involved, many of whom might not be local, there would quite likely be more crime or anti-social behaviour than with a purely rural population of agricultural workers.

Two views of the Muker court house.

The two pictures of the old Courthouse above are provided by courtesy of John Kilburn of Swale Farm Guest House and were kindly taken by John Severs on a visit in company with Paul Sherwood, who took the one alongside of the gaol. The latter may have been a handy lock-up for drunken offenders.

Muker Gaol.

Aldborough

David Lorrimer of Bradford, who had read a request in The Dalesman to contact the author with any information, kindly wrote to say .

"On a walk recently I came upon a delightful court house in the village of Aldborough, near Boroughbridge. The court house stands adjacent to the village green by the stocks.

There is a plaque saying that it is...............

The Old Court House of the Ancient borough of Aldborough and Boroughbridge of which members of Parliament were elected till 1832"

Photograph by
David Lorrimer

He later added that he had come across reference to the Blue Bell Inn at Arkendale, fairly close to Aldborough, having been used as a court house; and he mentioned in a book, *Arkendale, its Church and People,* reference was made to an inquest having taken place at the Blue Bell, after the death of a William Howard, when his leg was trapped in a threshing machine in March 1868., it being quoted .

.... *"At the inquest in the Blue Bell, the jury recommended that these machines should be made safer, as such accidents were common."*

These may not be courthouses lost in the 20th century changes but they are worth recording as part of the history of venues of justice in Yorkshire.

Tockwith

As with Aldborough, the court house at Tockwith was of an earlier vintage and its use as such did not continue into the more recent times, the last sitting being recorded in 1869. However, from a point of interest it is worth including, if only to record its place in the history of community law within the county.

The following will scarcely do justice to the comprehensive history by John Graham of Tockwith from which these notes are contrived.

The Toll Booth at Tockwith.
Picture taken from the Millennium book of Tockwith,
by kind permission of John Graham.

Dating from medieval times, known as the Toll Booth, the building which stands at the corner of Front Street and Long Street was the place where the Lord of the Manor collected fees from the traders using the market place. In those days it was only a single storey structure but it also had an important purpose as being the premises where the Court Leet was held. This was the criminal court for the district which had been granted directly to the Manor by the King. Its range of powers were wide, including most of what would today come before the justices, other than homicide; so not a lot has changed in all that time. Monetary values are somewhat different, as so many of those then recorded were in pence and shillings, so we can truly see how inflation has changed things over the centuries.

The Court had additional powers which regulated a number of matters relating to trade, such as the quality of the ale in the public houses, and it was the local equivalent of the modern weights and measures officers of any current local authority.

Those who took part in making the decisions were known as jurors and, as today, there was a clerk, then known as the Steward, for the court to transcribe the rulings and keep the records. Those papers are held to this day in the County Records of the East Riding at Beverley.

Although it is not known exactly, it seems that the Toll Booth was enlarged to two floors about the mid 16th century and as its similar cousins, the Moot Halls, it included places for traders to carry out their business, for a fee of payable to the Lord of the Manor.

This transition brought about the structure roughly as it can be seen today, and where the first floor provided the court or meeting room, whilst those who carried out trade functions had to be satisfied with the lower rooms on the street level. It is likely that there was also a town lock up to contain the naughty ones of the district.

By the end of the 18th century the junior Court Baron had been allowed to join the Court Leet in using the building, which by then was becoming known as The Court House and this continued until cessation of use in 1869.

Sittings at the premises varied to include Quarter Sessions, and in addition all manners of other meetings, such as would now be the task of a town or parish council took place. For those who failed to obey the rules laid down by the latter, levies known as pains had to be issued to the recalcitrant offenders.

When magistrates courts were first formalised in the 1840s it was not in Topcliffe where the choice of venue lay, and the meetings of the medieval courts had diminished to a bare once per annum. So the courts which had been so important for some many years ceased to be and the modern forebears of our present system of councils and magistrates courts were established on a wider geographical basis.

Despite this loss of control over its affairs Topcliffe had one distinctive feature to lift its importance above many other buildings around the country. It is said that it was at Topcliffe where a ransom was paid to the Scots for the release of Charles I. However, a more detailed investigation of the circumstances refutes that suggestion, the money having been counted out at Northallerton, although it certainly brings Tockwith into the complicated process of how the ransom was paid. Those who wish to read the whole tale should obtain a copy of the *Millennium Book of Topcliffe*.

After some interesting usages during the years after its use as a court ceased, including functioning as a canteen for servicemen during World War II, it was decided that the premises should be preserved and brought back to an acceptable standard for such an important relic of former times.

It had survived the whim of the County Council to demolish it in the 1960s when it had fallen on rather hard times, and since then it has been listed and put to very good use for the residents of the village. Thus the best of two worlds has preserved this historical building and brought it to a useful purpose in the present day.

How different that is from the places where such premises were put under the demolition hammer to make way for progress, and in many places that started in Victorian times, let alone what has gone on since then.

I am extremely grateful to John Graham of Tockwith for being so kind as to allow me to use the article and one of the pictures contained therein, as the basis for this short piece.

Bedale

Paul Sherwood mentioned to the author that a friend of his, Muriel Blythman, a retired JP who lives in Arrathorne near Bedale, commented to him recently, as follows.

"Just out of interest re Court Houses. I have been led to believe that the Farm next door to me, Cote House Farm, was used as a court in the 1700s. I used to know Mary Smith who died about 8 years ago and she took me around the house when I first got to know her in the early 1980s. She told me how the house (sitting room) was used for court proceedings and later used as a school for the local community".

In addition in former years they had the use of the clerk s office, at the police station, or at times the Savings Bank Building for occasional courts. The 1845 Return states that they met in the Public Room which was plainly part of the Poor House in the town as the magistrates paid a fee of 1 guinea each per annum to the Trustees for the Poor. Indictable offences would be heard on any day of the week.

Sadly, Bedale suffered a major makeover in the mid Victorian years. The old Tollbooth and many other buildings were demolished in favour of fine town houses , so there is no picture of the premises. The Poor House on the outskirts of the town is a later building and was not used as a court.

Bulmers Directory mentions that in 1890 the magistrates sat on alternate Tuesdays at 12 noon, in the Court House at the Town Hall which was built in 1840.

Interesting light is thrown on some types of cases in that a tramping labourer in 1899 was sentenced to 14 days hard labour with 7/- (35p) costs for vagrancy and refusing to work. This sentence is rather akin to the Morley case of fining an innkeeper for not having a cup of water at his door to refresh travellers. Would that present times could be so simple! However, events have progressed and in more recent times the Court House at Bedale was home to the Hang East Bench which normally met on a Tuesday at 10.00hrs.

The courthouse as pictured below was built in 1904, being one of those combined with a police station.

Paul Sherwood says *".. when I was appointed in '93 we used to sit at Stokesley, Thirsk, Bedale & Northallerton, until all the others shut. Richmond sat at Richmond & Leyburn".*

Bedale Courthouse.
Picture by courtesy of Paul Sherwood.

It continued to be used until it was closed as the Hang East justices combined with others to sit in Northallerton. The last day of sitting was on 19th December 1996.

Scorton

The 1845 return of petty sessions reports that the Gilling East justices sat in a room at the Black Bull without any charge being made. Presumably, as noted in other places, the custom brought to the house was sufficient to recompense the landlord for any problem of inconvenience. The clerk recording this was Wm Price of Scorton near Catterick.

Former premises of the Scorton Courts.
Picture by courtesy of Paul Sherwood.

Nothing more has come to light on this matter. Presumably justice moved to be served at Richmond.

Richmond

As a Borough in its own right the town had a Borough Court and it was reported in the petty session return of 1845 that it sat in the Common Hall. This was described as a room within a suite of rooms set up a flight of stairs adjacent to an Inn but normally kept self contained there-from.

Baines in 1823 states that the magistrates held their meeting every Monday morning, with no reference as to venue, but makes reference to Quarter Sessions being held in the Town Hall. This was built by Richmond Council in 1756 on the site of a much earlier guildhall, a purpose of the new building being to serve as a formal hall and for town pleasure purposes. He refers to *'balls, assemblies and public gaieties of the town'* as part of the functions held there.

Baines also refers to the town having its own Recorder, a Mr Wailes who had been appointed *vide* the Mayor and Aldermen. There is also reference to the Duke of Leeds as chief bailiff of the liberty of Richmond and its shire holding *'court for causes'* in the gaol, which he owned, where the matters under consideration did not amount to 40s(hillings)

In the 19th and 20th centuries the justices sat in the Town Hall.

Richmond Town Hall.
Picture by courtesy of Paul Sherwood.

The Gilling East and Hang West justices joined to sit as one bench in 1953. A new courthouse, not of endearing architecture as shown below, was opened.

Richmond Courthouse 20th century style
Picture by courtesy of Paul Sherwood.

On 21st March 2004 The Richmond Courthouse closed and the justices transferred to the refurbished Northallerton Courthouse.

The last sitting at Richmond Courthouse.
Picture by courtesy of Paul Sherwood.

Easingwold

Easingwold was the home of the Bulmer West justices. In 1845, according to the Return of Petty Sessions, they were sitting in a room at the George Inn, now the present well popular hotel.

Michael Riley, a director of the hotel, says that there is no trace of the room which was used.

The previous Oak Room, which was a possibility had been converted to new bedrooms some years ago.

The George Hotel.
Oopyright with George Hotel, shown by courtesy of Michael Riley.

Then for many years they sat in the Central Buildings on two days, being the second and last Wednesday in the month. This was augmented by meeting each Friday in the clerk s office, the venue of which is unknown.

Central Buildings, Easingwold.
Picture by Sheila Jefferson, courtesy of Paul Sherwood.

One can only presume that those sessions held in the Central Buildings were dealing with offenders within the district, and that the sittings in the comfort of the clerk s rooms dealt with other matters.

The bench later moved to sitting in the handsome Town Hall located then, as now, in the main market square.

Easingwold Town Hall.
Picture by Sheila Jefferson, courtesy of Paul Sherwood.

In the 1960s a new modern courthouse was built in the town to which all court work was transferred.

The 1960's style utilitarian Court House in Easingwold.
Picture by Sheila Jefferson, courtesy of Paul Sherwood.

As has been noted elsewhere, changes continued throughout the late 20th century as in many parts of the country Petty Sessional Divisions merged, either to suit the needs of the shifting communities or to satisfy the requirements of administrators under the directions of government. At Easingwold, instead of gathering in other benches to more utilise the new courthouse, the reverse took place.

The Bulmer bench was broken up in 1996 and divided three ways, to York, Northallerton and to the Ryedale Bench which sat at Pickering. The courthouse closed for the purpose of taking cases.

Ever mindful of the need to house the ever expanding courts administration, the new building continued to be active as the centre for the North Yorkshire Magistrates Courts Committee which had transferred there from their offices in Thirsk.

That situation has moved on again as the Courts Service for North Yorkshire is now housed at Northallerton.

Crayke

Mentioned in the Petty Sessional Return of 1845 is the Parish of Craike.(sic)

Although nearby to Easingwold, it was technically a detached part of County Durham, as the affairs were managed by the Principality and the Bishop of Durham.

The Durham Ox.

Sessions in 1845 were taken in a room of the Durham Ox by the Clerk for Easingwold, John Haxby.

In 1823, Edward Baines says that the magistrate was also the Rector, The Revd. P C A M Guise. It is unknown when it ceased to be used as a court room.

I am grateful to Michael Ibbotson, Managing Director of the Durham Ox, for permission to include this picture of the premises, which nowadays are noted for fine cuisine rather than petty sessions.

Helmsley

The 1845 Petty Session Return notes from the Clerk, Robert Petch of Kirkby Moorside, record that the sessions in Helmsley were held in The Black Swan Inn.

In the *History of Helmsley,* compiled by local historians, it is mentioned that the old Toll Booth was first opened in 1642, but in 1802 the first floor became a private school. Later in 1857 this was The Court House, with the County Court Offices on the lower floor.

This building was succeeded on the same site by the Town Hall, opened in 1901, which then housed the Court, although in 1908 it is recorded that one room of the building was made over for use as a reading room and library.

Not listed amongst the ones used in recent times, the Court House at Helmsley was a feature of the Town Hall.

Picture by courtesy of Paul Sherwood.

My helpful contact in North Yorkshire, Paul Sherwood, tells me that the landlord, William aged about 80, of the Sun Inn at Bilsdale recalls . *"Ah, they were still sitting there in 1953, used to alternate between Kirkby Moorside & Helmsley, Lady Feversham was on the bench, three women and two men, Colonel ?? (he remembered, I forgot) was a difficult..(edited).. chairman. Certain it was 1953, I had just bought my first car in late 1952 and I remember taking my mother to court for a license not long after......"*

Enquiries to date have not managed to ascertain just when court business ceased to be conducted in Helmsley, nor to where the cases were taken thereafter.

This may have been around the time of the 1974 evolutions and as Helmsley was an alternative venue with Kirkby Moorside, either Malton or Pickering may have been the first stopover before final departure to Scarborough.

Thirsk

The last building to be used as a Magistrates Court in Thirsk was the Courthouse, built in 1885. It was adjacent to the police office and latterly also housed the Justices Clerk s Office.

Its function in all these capacities ceased in 1997 when the court work transferred to Northallerton court with the clerks, but the Justices Chief Executive with the courts administration moved to the Easingwold premises.

The County Court had previously closed in 1936.

Moving even further back in time the Birdforth justices had managed their business in 1867 by sitting at the Thirsk Police Station and it is presumed that this practice ceased in 1885 with the opening of the new Court building.

The former Courthouse, a very handsome building, has now been sympathetically restored and houses an Arts Centre.

The Old Courthouse at Thirsk.

Picture by courtesy of Paul Sherwood.

Northallerton

There is some early history of courts in Northallerton which is worth noting.

Going way back to 1344 there is mention of a moot hall or toll booth and various courts, Moot Courts, the Manor Courts and the Halmote courts for Bishop of Durham, Chief Bailiff for the Liberty of Hallamshire, followed in due course by the Quarter Sessions for the North Riding, then from the 19th century the Magistrates Courts for Allertonshire.

Housing these over the centuries has been the task of several premises. From 1344 a Toll Booth was used, which is depicted on the right of the following sketch, but it is not known if this was the original building or a rebuild over the years.

Market Place with Toll Booth.

Picture by courtesy of Colin Narramore.

The picture immediately following is described variously as the site of the Old Guildhall drawing attention to the fact that it was later the workhouse.

Others say that the building behind the lamppost was in fact the Guildhall, with only a purpose and name change to being the Workhouse.

Whatever was the case, it was eventually demolished.

Picture by courtesy of Colin Narramore.

The plaque to the left is on the present building on the site depicted below.

Pictures alongside and below courtesy of Paul Sherwood.

A new building was erected, now occupied by solicitors.

Paul Sherwood remarks that the whole area has been redeveloped.

The old view shows Sun Beck which ran alongside a road with a bridge on the High Street, where a roundabout is now set. Sun Beck ended up being put in a culvert during the 1950s-70s.

During the period from 1720, until 1770, Vine House on the opposite side of the road became the home for the Sessions.

The premises later housed Rutson Hospital as shown overleaf with the descriptive plaque, but in 2008 the rehabilitation services provided were transferred to the Friary Hospital.

Vine House

Pictures by courtesy of Paul Sherwood,

Our old friend the Toll Booth then re-emerged as the venue for the dispossessed sessions which continued to be held there until 1785. It then became a general purpose building, for functions which have not been ascertained, before being demolished in 1873. In 1872 the plans for a Town Hall were passed and this was built and opened by 1873.

The new Town Hall building shown here was a little further away from the cross than its predecessor the Toll Booth.

Picture by courtesy of Colin Narramore.

Events had taken a significant turn in 1784 when worthies decided to build a new Sessions House which was opened in 1785 on East Road; taking its place amongst other fine buildings constructed in Yorkshire onwards into a century of Victorian development.

Picture taken by George Martin of Northallerton Camera Club in 1956, and provided by courtesy of the North Yorkshire County Records Office.

Northallerton Sessions House 1956

Baines in his 1823 book relates that the North Riding Quarter Sessions and the Bishop of Durham s Manor and Halmote courts were held *'in the court house situated on the east side of the town where also lay the House of Correction',* that being the gaol said to be able to house up to 100 prisoners. He then reports that the magistrates for Allertonshire sat weekly on Wednesdays. The use of the name magistrate is interesting here, as until somewhat over a decade later they were often just called justices .

We move on then to 1845 and the Return of Petty Sessions to Parliament submitted by the Clerk, Mr Henry Hirst of Northallerton. In this document it is stated that the court venue for the Allertonshire magistrates is *'The magistrates' room (for the said North Riding), attached to and communicating with the Court House',* thus implying that the venue for the magistrates was an extra room attached to the original building.

Whatever the case, the premises were rebuilt in 1880, but where the courts were held in the meantime is not known, possibly the Town Hall. Thereafter the courts remained in the Sessions House until the present premises were built in 1936 and opened in 1937 as the new courthouse. The Sessions House was then used for other purposes, including by the Fire Brigade, but it was demolished in the early 1990s and the site remains vacant.

The current Northallerton Magistrates' Courthouse in 2008.
Picture by courtesy of Paul Sherwood.

During its period of service there have been some changes. In 1969 or thereabouts, as a result of a Beeching Report the courthouse ceased to be used for Quarter Sessions and Assizes, all of which transferred to the new system of Crown Courts, being removed to Middlesbrough into a purpose built court building.

The Northallerton premises were then adapted so that some of the spare space could be used as administrative offices by the County Council. The Allertonshire magistrates however remained the main user with occasional use by Darlington County Court or the Coroner.

Opening Ceremony 2004.
Picture taken by Richard Jemison
Provided by courtesy of Paul Sherwood.

On evacuation by all other people, leaving only the courts, in 2003 the premises were re-furbished, with HRH The Duke of York re-opening them in 2004.

The premises are now home to all the benches which have, as described on other pages, been merged to form the Northallerton and Richmond Bench, including Thirsk, Richmond, Stokesley, Bedale, Leyburn and parts of the Easingwold District.

In addition the offices of Her Majesty s Court Service, North Yorkshire, are accommodated.

Greta Bridge

As has been mentioned in various parts of this book, at times some courts sat in rather informal surroundings. One such case in the 19th century was when the Morritt Arms at Greta Bridge on the A66, south of Barnard Castle, served as a court venue for the Gilling West Bench.

This was not the premises now known as The Morritt Arms but others on the South East side of the bridge which had been built by the Morritt family in the late 19th century. The landlord of the time renamed it The George. It subsequently was closed.

The former Morritt Arms at Greta Bridge.
Picture courtesy of Paul Sherwood.

They can not have been over burdened with cases as the first Tuesday in each month was sufficient to deal with the work. It is recorded that by 1929 they were sitting on the last Wednesday of the month in Barnard Castle, County Durham.

As is previously noted they transferred to Richmond Town Hall, but that did not stop them taking occasional courts in the police station or sessions at the clerk s office.

Malton and Norton

The author will no doubt be reprimanded by the purists as, whereas Malton is a market town from the North Riding now in North Yorkshire, Norton was in the East Riding; but as the two are now part of the same grouping in North Yorkshire, set apart only by the river Derwent, with Malton being the name most widely used by the people passing through or around on their way to the coast, I have opted for ease and am listing them here, together.

No doubt, as with many other places, justice in earliest times was meted out by local justices in makeshift courtrooms in their houses or possibly in an inn or two.

By 1845 a return made to the House of Commons by clerks, Alfred & William Simpson of New Malton, notes that magistrates for the Buckrose Division of the East Riding County sat in New Malton in the North Riding of Yorkshire *"in a building called the Town Hall, the property of the Right Hon Earl Fitzwilliam. Petty Sessions are sometimes held for the district at the Railway Hotel in Norton within the division; but this is only of rare occurrence, the usual place of holding the same being in the Town Hall .*

The New Malton Market Hall shown above was enlarged and refronted in 1856, when the commercial units below were covered in, giving greater status to the Town Hall portion of the building. In 1857 there was a fire in the building, and the picture on the right shows the Town Hall portion after refurbishment.

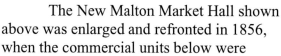

Pictures provided by courtesy of John Stone.

The Railway Hotel in Wold Street, Norton.
Originally known as the Bay Horse until 1850, it has subsequently changed its name again to The Railway Tavern.

Picture by courtesy of John Stone.

The matter then gets more complex as in April 1855 we are told that *"the sanction of the East Riding Magistrates has been given to the plan for the execution of a Lock-Up and Magistrates Room at Norton, we understand they will be built upon a piece of ground which belongs to the Riding near the bridge"*.

"The Court House was built in 1855 on the site of a large garden. It had a court, magistrates' rooms, superintendent's residence and two cells. This then served the Buckrose division. Later, on closure, the premises were occupied by Mr J H Wise, then Miss Masterman had a young ladies school, and she was followed by a Miss Miller who also conducted a young ladies seminary".

"On 13th January 1909 the Old Police Station opened as a Parish Room for St Peter's Guild. It had been in disuse since 1902".

"Mr Charles Bower's Garage (1921) (which) was formerly Norton Police Station and Court House, contains rooms for the use of the superintendent of police, a lock-up, the county magistrates met here on the first and third Saturdays in each month. To hear a case you had to stand as the only seat available was a bench fixed round the walls of the room".

190

The premises, which were on Commercial Street are shown on the following pictures after their conversion to a garage in 1921. The rear view below shows the extent of the premises.

All pictures by courtesy of John Stone.

Meanwhile, in 1900 the Town Hall in Malton had given way to this fine Court House and Police Station which can be viewed on the left of Victoria Road in the scene below.

This was built in Yorkshire Stone with columns of polished Aberdeen granite, included a court room and a magistrates retiring room and was opened in 1901.

Likewise in Norton there had been further changes which had brought about the disuse as a courthouse of the premises which later became the garage. In 1902 new premises, probably to the design of Alfred Beaumont the County Surveyor, were built on Commercial Street on the opposite side of the road to the 1855 buildings.

A view shows down Commercial Street the 1902 court building set back first on the left. The police station in red brick is next. This is followed by the premises of a high street, shops, houses and offices.

Picture courtesy of John Stone.

Together with the Court House in Malton these dealt with justice in the twin towns until 1974, when the latter was closed.

Thereafter magistrates for Malton (Ryedale Division) sat in the courthouse on Commercial Street, Norton, until it was decreed that such buildings with minimum facilities would no longer serve the purpose in the 20th century. The justices were decamped to sit with other colleagues in a variety of other places, and the building closed for courts purposes.

Happily it remains as the office for the Norton Town Council, and the courthouse building as pictured overleaf in 2008 is used as the council chamber.

The author is greatly obliged to Mr John Stone, a lifetime resident of the area for the above pictures from his large collection, and for the quoted comments preceding them.

Roger King, a former Norton Town Clerk, wrote to the author . *"I don't now remember the exact year but in the late 1990s the courthouse (then nearing 100 years old) was closed and the site, including the police station, put up for sale by North Yorkshire County Council. It was bought by Ryedale Housing Association (now part of Yorkshire Housing) which submitted plans to Ryedale District Council to redevelop the site for housing, leaving the Town Council's accommodation intact in the old police station but, crucially, including a plan to convert the courthouse into two dwellings.*

The Town Council was opposed to the latter and subsequently negotiated with the Housing Association to lease the Courthouse as the Council Chamber and office, with its former accommodation incorporated into the proposed housing. Thus, the Courthouse, with its magistrates' bench, dock, witness box and legal benches has been preserved".

The 1902 Courthouse in Norton, where the Rydale Bench sat until cases were transferred to Pickering in 1998, and ultimately to Scarborough.

Picture taken by the author.

Tony Hemesley, a Malton magistrate both before and during this period of change, recalls some uniquely interesting matters about the court

"Our local courtroom at Norton was a gem of the Victorian period; almost impossible to work in as there were no Retiring Rooms and we either had to decamp to the Clerk of Norton Council's Office or the Norton Council Chamber".

193

"For simple decisions we sometimes sat on the steps behind the heavy green baize door. That was very convenient as the defendant's cell was on the way back into court. On occasion the more local of our clients would give us a nice smile on the way back to business."

Picture taken by the author.

The wording Police Court is still clearly visible over the front door. Nowadays such obvious links between police and justices are not considered to be appropriate.

Tony continues *"At lunch we went across the road to the Cornucopia pub where the Magistrates, Solicitors, Witnesses and defendants all had their own allotted areas. We were served according to the need to get back into court in a hurry, so the magistrates always got their lunch last. This system always worked."*

When the court house closed, the magistrates worked with other colleagues and would sit varyingly at the Pickering, Whitby or Scarborough courts. In 2010 only the last named venue remains as an active courthouse. Thus, within a period of little more than a decade, as in other places, the work of the justices, which had previously merited two courts in substantial buildings in the twin towns for more than a century and a half, had been merged to a role of anonymity in a distant seaside spa town.

Flaxton

In 1845, according to the Petty Sessional Return, the Bulmer justices Northern Division were sitting in the Lobster House, near to Flaxton, which was a notable Inn on the side of the present A64 road, about eight miles from York.

This practice was certainly in place at the time of the Revd Sydney Smith s incumbency at Thornton le Clay, from 1809, as noted by the well known historian J P G (Sam) Taylor in his correspondence with the author. It is not quite clear when this ceased to be the case.

The former Lobster House Inn.
Now a private farm.

Author's picture.

Note: St John Pilkington comments to the author re Flaxton   .

.... I think that it had a courthouse other than the pub as various directories has Bulmer East sitting at 'The Sessions House'. The wording in the 1893 Kellys Directory is not clear but seems to imply that the Sessions House was the Reading Room which was erected in 1892.

Is that the room now effectively used as the Village Hall?"

Kirkbymoorside

As with so many other places the ancient Courts Baron and Leet courts were the fore-runners of present day justice, the former for matters of title and other civil rights, and the latter for criminal matters. In respect of the former, the cases were heard by a bailiff or steward with twelve local citizens acting as jurors who were meant to control any excess of power imposed by the local lord.

Justices, predecessors of magistrates, sat for the Court Leet and, like many other towns, Kirkbymoorside had its own stocks and pillory to deal with offenders. These were in evidence as late as 1870. In these crime ridden days many mourn their passing.

By 1823 that latter court in the town had put in place a constable, by name of William Newton. Those apprehended by him would be locked up in the hoppit , the cells beneath the main building of the magnificent Toll Booth. The magistrates only sat on a monthly basis, so some miscreants could have spent a fair time in custody for their sins before being tried.

The Toll Booth, Kirkbymoorside, re-built in 1871.

Picture by Robin Butler, provided
by courtesy of Louise Mudd.

I am grateful to Louise Mudd for further explanations ..

"There has been a public hall on the site of the Toll Booth since the 17th century and so has undergone a few changes from its original form. The building seen today replaced an older public hall structure and was rebuilt from stone scavenged from a ruined hunting lodge (Neville Castle) at the top of the town. This lodge had fallen into disuse and in 1730 part of it was pulled down and the Toll Booth built in the town's centre from the stone. It originally had 30 different rooms over 3 storeys and the cellar ("The Hoppit") was used a lock up until 1851 when the police station and two cells were built. The Toll Booth was burnt down in 1871 and rebuilt as a two storey building. It was bought in 1920 from the Feversham Estate by the residents of Kirkbymoorside and is now run by a management committee and .... called the Kirkbymoorside War Memorial Hall".

No doubt, as in many other places, the upper rooms of the Toll Booth held the court when the justices sat to consider cases, and it would be used for the various other town administrative duties. It is remarked that the true interpretation of the word toll is prison, thus suggesting that the penalty for misdemeanour was a toll , nothing to do with any other dues which might be payments for other purposes. Interestingly the lower level is filled in, when in other places it was left open for traders to hawk their wares, which might have been the case with the original buildings.

In 1845 the sessions were reported as being held in the King s Head in the town. By 1856 the North Yorkshire Police Force was established and a police station with two cells which had been built in the town in 1851 on Tinley Garth was in operation. The local magistrates had the foresight to build a police station with a secure prison four years before a countywide force came into being. A Petty Sessions court sat on Market Days, alternating with Helmsley, and in the early days the really serious cases would then proceed to Sessions at York.

The Duncombe family held the position of Chairman of the Bench, with Lord Feversham for Helmsley and Kirbymoorside Petty

Sessions and Quarter Sessions. In the early 20th century chairmanship of the bench passed out of the family other than when appointed.

The police house and police station on Tinley Garth which had been built in 1851, preceding the formation of the official police force in North Yorkshire.

A cell is clearly visible and subject of a preservation order by being listed.

Picture taken by and courtesy of Louise Mudd.

Church House, where courts were held during the 1939-45 war years
Picture taken by and courtesy of Louise Mudd.

The Church House was used as a courthouse during World War II on a needs basis, as the Army frequently used the former Toll

Booth, which had been renamed as the Memorial Hall after 1919 in recognition of those who died in World War I, for lectures etc., and military needs took priority.

The author is extremely grateful to Louise Mudd and the Kirkbymoorside History Project Group for the provision of all the pictures, and for the valuable information in this short piece which is taken from the considerable article produced in the Kirkbymoorside Times in 2004 copyrighted to The Kirkbymoorside History Project.

It is helpful people in valuable groups such as this which have made the task of discovering the lost courthouses , so pleasurable; quite apart from the very valuable work they do in keeping records of their local antiquities and history.

Pickering

The first Court dealt with Forest Laws. They were held twice a year in the Courthouse in the Castle Grounds, and these were the Courts Leet, as with Danby and in other places, to protect the Duchy of Lancaster s lands.

By 1845 the Return made by Thomas Bainton of Pickering notes that the Petty Sessions for Pickering Lyth (East) were held alternately in the Black Swan Inn and the White Swan Inn, a small sum being paid for the rent of the rooms.

Betty Hood, a former magistrate, told the author about the Police Station and Justice Room (or Court House) in Eastgate which was built in 1878 and was very imposing, it had cells. 12 Magistrates (County) sat every month.

The copy accompanying the picture below states *"This wrinkled old photograph, glued onto canvas, is unique as it shows Pickering Police Station, courthouse and cells at the bottom of Kirkham Lane. Also pictured is the butchers shop which later became Kitty Burrells cafe. All these buildings, along with Wilf McNeils house and the blacksmiths shop, were demolished to widen the road and improve access to RAF Fylingdales early warning station during its construction in the early1960's"*.

The Old Courthouse.
Permission for the use of this picture from the
Sidney Smith Collection is given by the copyright holders
'The Beck Isle Museum Trust and Mrs. Barbara Sokel'

The new Courthouse built then in Malton Road served the area until 2006 when it was closed after consolidation decisions, and all court business was transferred to Scarborough.

The more modern Pickering courthouse shows little of architectural quality.
Author's picture.

In this piece about Pickering the author is especially grateful for the help received from former magistrate Elizabeth (Betty) Hood, and to Rodge Dowson and colleagues at the Beck Isle Museum.

Visitors to the town are well advised to visit the museum which is well provided with information about the life and times of the various citizens of Pickering and the immediate area around the town. Local museums can tend to give a deeper and more personal picture of the people and events which shaped the towns of Britain than some of the wider based regional or national enterprises.

Whitby

Whitby had a Toll Booth from earlier times, belonging to the Abbey. In the Victoria County History *The History of the County of York and the North Riding of Yorkshire* mention is made that in 1640 this was replaced by a Toll Booth erected in the Market Place. This also served as a Correction House and Court House with a small prison, known as a *hoppet*(sic), beneath. In 1788 this was replaced with a new Town Hall in which the manorial courts were held. Now, as the Old Town Hall, the building still has pride of place on Market Street.

Like many others in Britain it had a main hall above and an open space below. The latter would be used by traders, but the first floor room would have been reserved for town matters and dealing with the law. It is typical of the period, many elsewhere in former years being known as Moot Halls, but being a Victorian structure the new name, Town Hall, was applied in Whitby.

This fine view of the Old Whitby Town Hall, taken by the author shows the similarity to much older Moot Halls. Holiday makers would not be unlike the bustle of traders in the earlier years of its existence.

Around 1817 there is mention of some cases being heard at the home of Richard Moorsom, Airy Hill.

Justice matters were at some yet un-discovered date moved to premises on Flowergate where there was a room for the magistrates and a small prison beneath.

These premises remain, and it is said that the old cell is still there, but the author decided that he did not want to be locked up , so the picture displays only the building exterior.

Picture by courtesy of the owner of Bagshawes
April 2009.

These imposing premises on Flowergate are referred to in the 1845 return which reports the justices sat in the offices of Butcher and Buchannan solicitors.

The room was furnished by courtesy and could be denied to them at any time.

The building was later occupied by Bagshawe, another local solicitor.

In 2009 it was a cafØ, named Bagshawes .

A new Police Station was built later in the century, described as being just off Baxter Gate . This would appear to be the premises on Spring Hill, a road which started a mere 165 feet from Baxtergate, where the magistrates sat in a room at the front of the building holding petty sessions on Tuesdays and Fridays and on other occasional days.

The room was also used as a County Court once a month. There were four cells at the rear of the building.

Interestingly, on Baxtergate, at No 23 was the house of John Buchannan, a solicitor, who had the Flowergate premises which are mentioned above as being used as court premises.

It is worth showing a picture of the Baxtergate premises which of themselves look to be imposing enough to serve as a courthouse.

Author's picture by courtesy of North Yorkshire Law.

The premises on Spring Hill are shown below to the right of picture house.

The picture on the left is by John Tindall and is shown here by courtesy of the Whitby Literary and Philosophical Society, also acknowledging the assistance of Christiane Kroebel the Hon. Librarian and Archivist.

If any one can locate a full frontal of those premises which comprised a Police Station with a courthouse room it would be useful to be able to add them to the archives in the town.

The picture on the right, kindly taken by David Pybus in 2009 shows the site of the later demolished premises on Spring Hill.

The Bench continued to conduct its sittings at this old Police Station on Spring Hill, prior to it being demolished during the 1960 s. A new police station was built but the magistrates did not sit there as it was no longer deemed correct for the two to be together.

However, before 1973, whilst the new courthouse was being built, business was conducted in the Whitby Urban District Council Chambers which were in St Hilda s Terrace, Whitby.

This picture of the very handsome council buildings was taken by David Pybus in 2009.

The 1991 Ordnance Survey of the town clearly shows the new premises on Waterstead Lane, shown overleaf, and it was there, from 1973, that the cases were brought before local magistrates until further government inspired changes later on brought consolidation with the courts of Malton, Pickering and Scarborough.

Whitby Courthouse on Waterstead Lane.

Picture by David Pybus.

Although the magistrates court business was transferred to Scarborough in 1998 the building did not close.

This was just as well, because in 2004-5 when the 1970s Scarborough Courts were being re-furbished the justices returned to Whitby for a spell. However by 2006 they were back in Scarborough.

That was the end of a few centuries of local justice being held in Whitby. Latterly the building served purely for the County Court and hardly ever as a magistrates court.

In 2009, official notice has been given for the courthouse to be formally closed, it being felt that the occasional use by the County Court does not merit the premises being retained, and that the cases for that court can be taken in Scarborough.

I am extremely grateful to David Pybus of Whitby for his help, together with the Whitby Literary and Philosophical Society, in assisting me to understand magisterial affairs in the town. Without such help here, and from other kind people in parts of Yorkshire, this document would scarcely be more than a small pamphlet.

Scarborough

In Baines 1823 *History and Gazetteer of the North Riding of Yorkshire* reference is made to the Town Hall of Scarborough being a spacious building situated on Long Room Street and the Sessions were held there.

By 1845 the Parliamentary return of Sessions made for Pickering-by-the-East by Edward Devner of Scarborough stated quite simply that the sessions were held in The Borough Town Hall.

This picture, is of premises which in the late 1700s changed from a private house to being the Assembly Rooms and then the Borough Town Hall. They were situated on Long Room Street, now St Nicholas Street.

After 1899, on vacation of the premises to the newer Town Hall a few yards down the street, Lloyds Bank took over until their merger of TSB and further move in the late 20th century.

Author's picture, 2009.

The courts then moved to a courthouse, previously a prison, on Castle Road / St Thomas Street, but this was vacated around 1964 when the new premises were provided in the present location on Northway.

I am indebted to Kevin Page, Clerk to the Justices for kind permission to show this old picture on the next page.

The Old Court House, in the right foreground.
View taken looking down Castle Road with St Thomas Street on the right.

Picture held in the Courthouse, Scarborough
Originally sourced by Max Payne.

That Court House was demolished circa 1971. The current Courthouse, shown below, was updated and modified in 2003-4 in order to accommodate all the cases which had arrived from Malton, Pickering and Whitby in the preceding years.

The Northway Courthouse in 2009.
Picture taken by the author.

As the matter of a former prison on Castle Road has come into the tale it would be useful to add a little further information on the various gaols which have been part of the scene over the years.

First of all the Castle with its dungeons was the main gaol for criminals and others who had failed in their duty to society, but this was followed by a move to Newborough Bar circa 1640. That venue continued to be used until about 1840 when new premises were built on Castle Road but they had a short life, last being used for that purpose in 1866, when they were turned over to be used as a police station and Court House, as noted above.

In the previous year an entirely new custom built prison was built in Dean Road, which took over from Castle Road, and that continued to be used until 1878 when an Act of Parliament took prisons away from local authority control.

Wykeham

On the road from Malton to Scarborough lies the village of Wykeham which is within the ambit of the Dawnay Estates, and in that village is the Downe Arms, a hotel of some note and quality.

The Return of Petty Sessions in 1845 adds a dimension to its history, as in that year a gentleman by name of Edward S Devner of Scarborough reports that Petty Sessions for part of Pickering-by-the-East, for which he acted as Clerk as he did in Scarborough, were held in the Inn, no charge being levied for that purpose.

In 2009 neither the present Lady Downe nor the present Agent for the estates, Robert Sword, have any knowledge of such matters; the latter however notes that he believes from hearsay that the inn *building was originally a farmhouse and was then converted to a pub called the Black Bull. The family only moved to Wykeham Abbey in about 1905, and I believe that previously the Estate had been let".*

The Downe Arms pictured on the left in 2009 shows the frontage such as it might have been in 1845 other than the modern street lamp. There is a more modern extension to the left end.

There is no evidence as to which room might have been used as the courtroom.

Pictured provided by the Downe Arms and shown by their courtesy and of the Dawnay Estates.

It is possible that investigations into Dawnay Archives at the County Hall may add to this information.

North East of the North Riding

Teesside

There has been so much change in this area over the years that it is worth dealing with in its own section, with the following sketch map highlighting the area.

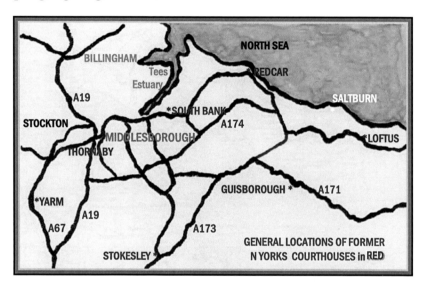

The first point to note is that Middlesbrough which now dominates the district was a relatively new comer, as it arose through the fast development of the steel and other allied industries in the 19th and 20th centuries.

In 1800 the place was a small hamlet, but by 1846 it had a Town Hall and in 1855 received its charter. From then on the place just grew as the main industrial centre of the Tees.

The towns of Guisborough, Yarm, and Stokesley, were until then the main centres in the area, with the additional developments of Loftus, Saltburn and Redcar growing throughout the 19th century. All were in the North Riding but the manipulations of officialdom and politicians in the 20th century changed all that. Via new counties of Teeside and Cleveland we have eventually arrived at the position that they all again reside in the Ceremonial County of North Yorkshire.

It takes more than a few administrators to tear away a section of Yorkshire. Strong connections remain with other coastal towns in the area, as residents of that part of the traditional county contribute much to the success of Whitby and Scarborough.

Those interested in these transient moves of boundaries must now refer elsewhere as we turn to consider how magistrates courts served the area. In this I am greatly indebted to Si n Jones, Clerk to the Justices at Middlesbrough, and information in the 1993 book by Malcolm Race JP to mark the 25th Anniversary of Teesside Bench *Six into one will go.*

Reference to the list of Wapentakes will show the two named as Langbaurgh East based on Guisborough and Langbaurgh West with its centre at Stokesley, and these were the traditional court areas which emerged and functioned for many years. Until April 2011 there was a Langbaurgh East bench sitting at Guisborough. Malcolm Race also refers to Langbaurgh North sitting at South Bank in his booklet on the subject.

The 1845 Return of Petty Sessions makes reference to sessions at Guisborough in the Toll Booth, belonging to a gentleman by name of Robert Chaloner, and those for Stokesley in the National School Room. For the division of Yarm the sessions were held in a *'room called the Town's Hall'*, evidently owned by the lord of the manor.

However over the years those venues were to be changed as increasing population required more commodious premises. In addition the developed towns acquired their own courts, but these have now gone with late 20th century rationalisation to major units.

Until the 1949 Justices of the Peace Act, some premises were shared with the police so those buildings reflected that dual purpose.

As with all the other benches in this area, there has been a lot of shuffling about over the latter part of the 20th century as counties were created then amended, then further altered. In the following notes I shall try to explain the changes which have taken place.

Stokesley

In Baines Directory of 1823 reference is made to Langbaurgh wapentake court in ancient times sitting at

"Langbargh, in the parish of Ayton, wap, and liberty of Langbargh; 3 mls NE of Stokesley, a ridge of rocks, where it is supposed the wapentake courts were anciently held, and whence this wapentake is denominated".

However accurate this may or may not be about courts being held in the open air this changed in later years, as there is an interesting note in *Stokesley Selection* (see footnote*) that .

"The Court was usually held in Stokesley in the old 'Town House' but later in the courtroom of the new Town Hall. In emergency the Court could meet at the private residence of the local JP. At Ingleby Arncliffe and at Stokesley Rectory there was a 'Court Room' incorporated in the residence".

In the same book further reference is made in a report of 1837 regarding the Police Force, where it is said ..

"At that time and previously all misdemeanours were heard at Stokesley's old 'Town House' (demolished in 1853)...........

Stokesley Toll Booth
Sketch by courtesy of Estelle Scott

213

.... *all cases coming from Middlesbrough, Marton, part of Thornaby and every village in Langbar coming within this jurisdiction; the bench was mainly composed of the local landowners and clergy".*

Estelle Scott who drew the above sketch says *"I'm attaching the toll booth drawing featuring William M. Duck Chemist, and Druggist,* (the shop) *who appears in the 1861 census. In 1841 the little shop was owned (or rented?) by William Kitching a Hatter who, inevitably, died of mercury poisoning".*

The 1845 Return states that Petty Sessions were held in the National School, William Garbutt, a solicitor in the town being noted as the clerk. The notes add that £2.2s is paid each year to the trustess for the use of the room, 3s.6d per meeting was paid to the laundress for the use of chairs, tables, a fire and cleaning the room in winter, but only 3s in the summer, noting that this rent averages 5s per session.

In the next picture, which appears in *Stokesley Selection* by Alec Wright and John Mawer, the small building with the castellated gutter is the Preston Grammar School.

The National School is the larger building to the right rear.
Picture included by kind permission of Peter Wood former owner of the publishers, Studio Print.

Joe Richardson of Stokesley Pride who has been most helpful in this matter, told the author that there are various dates for the provision of the National School dating from 1787, but the building shown was erected in 1811. He also notes that the building to the front was built in 1877 as an infant school.

So, having vacated the old Town House or Toll Booth, the Langbaurgh West justices seem to have held court in the National School for a period before moving to the comfort of the new Stokesley Town Hall, which was .

.another of the proud Victorian civic structures which had been built in 1853 as a gift to the town from Robert Hildyard.

Stokesley Town Hall.
Picture by courtesy of Paul Sherwood.

TOWN HALL
REPLACED OLDER TOWN HOUSE
AND TOLL BOOTH, ERECTED BY
COLONEL R. HILDYARD
IN 1853.
ORIGINALLY THIS HAD AN OPEN
ARCADE (BUTTER MARKET)
AT THE REAR ·

The 1866 Stokesley Directory, quoted in *Stokesley Selection*, states that Petty Sessions were held every Saturday, naming four of the justices and two clerks. Further notes remark that many of the cases were for drunkenness or wandering, both of which must have been a result of the social conditions of the time as unemployed men from elsewhere moved to look for work in the rising industrial areas adjacent to the Tees.

Assaulting the constable, which was a quite common offence brought a month s hard labour, abuse of animals or minor theft were other cases. In those days the fines of a few pence or shillings would seem quite large. On the other hand, for a male resident of the workhouse to take off wearing the clothes provided was a sin which earned him three months hard labour. Offences which imposed upon any of the town notables might attract a rather more severe penalty; all might not have been as even handed as the law dictates.

The court work must have been depleted by the formation of the bench at Middlesbrough in 1857, because until that new borough bench was formed, the residents of that town, as noted above, had to attend the sessions at Stokesley.

However, no doubt as the work of the council required more space in the Town Hall, the magistrates moved out to Stokesley Hall, also known as the Manor House, situated on the East of the Market Place.

Stokesley Hall, where the court was held in an upstairs room above the County Library until 31st December 1997 when it seems that all the work went to Northallerton.

Stokesley Hall.
Picture by courtesy of Paul Sherwood .

Amongst the people mentioned in this piece, together with Paul Sherwood, I am particularly grateful to Joe Richardson of Stokesley Pride who has helped me to pull together the various items mentioned above.

(* Stokesley Selection, collected by Alec Wright and John Mawer, published by Studio Print of Great Ayton in 1982. Extracts and pictures being by kind permission of Peter Wood, former owner of the copyright holder, Studio Print) .

Guisborough

Guisborough survived as a court venue, but not without its own fair share of change. Basically it was made up from the old Redcar & Saltburn and Guisborough benches. As noted to the author by Si n Jones it was based on previous local governm ent boundaries of 1968 which were not co-terminus with present local government or police boundaries. Further, it gathered in case work from Redcar, Grangetown, Dormanstown and Eston. All these were technically in the Teesside Local Justice area. Former South Bank work resided with Guisborough for a while but went back to Teeside in 2008.

The town is of considerable historical interest, allegedly by some to date back to Roman times, but at least it is listed in the Domesday Book and the ancient priory of *Gisborough* dates back to the 12th century, and the town was the centre of the Langbaurgh East wapentake, from which the session area takes its name.

The town had a Toll Booth which, as with other places, must have held the earlier sessions, it being mentioned that a manorial court was held once a year, but in 1821 the Town Hall, was erected on the site of the Toll Booth and it is recorded in some histories of the town that Petty Sessions were held every alternate Tuesday for East Langbaurgh.

There also appears to be some ancient knowledge that at one time the justices had sat in the Cock Inn, in the Market Place, later replaced by the National Westminster Bank building, before the construction of the Town Hall.

There is a curious disparity in dates here, as the Return of Petty Sessions for 1845 clearly states that the sessions were held in *'the Toll Booth, the private property of Robert Chaloner Esq.,* this being vouched for by T. Tudor Trevor the Clerk.

It is left to assumption that the new building retained the old name for a period and that the dignity of naming it as Town Hall was a later way of signifying the importance of the town.

The Town Hall
Built in 1821
which served
as the courthouse
for Langbaurgh East
through a large part
of the 19th and most
of the 20th centuries.

Picture taken and shown
by courtesy of Geoff Smith.

The Town Hall continued to act as the courts venue until the new courthouse, shown below, was built in 1968 However, Edgar Winfield, a former Court Clerk now living in Guisborough says via Malcolm Race that as the lease on the Town Hall ran out before the new courts were complete, the magistrates had to sit in the Church Hall. The new premises were extended in 1974.

The late
20th century
courthouse
shown here
would seem to
provide a sort
of helter-skelter
for the disabled.

Picture taken and shown here by c

The magistrates sat in Guisborough on four days of each week, having gathered in work from areas covered by closed courts; with only late arrests after 1pm on Fridays, and Saturdays, and domestic violence trials, going to Teeside court at Middlesbrough.

However by 2010 it had been decreed that the premises would close and all work be moved to the Teesside court in Middlesbrough.

In the words of Si n Jones, Cle rk to the Justices . *"The boiler broke down in December 2009 and with the consultation on courthouse closures pending, we moved the Langbaurgh East Bench to sit in a courtroom in Teesside from November 2010 until the fate of Guisborough was resolved. The decision has now been made to close it, so the LE bench will merge with Teesside in January 2012, and Guisborough will not be used again, save possibly a single valedictory sitting"*.

Loftus

Loftus Town Hall was built by the Earl of Zetland, erected by Mr Thomas Dickenson of Saltburn, and was first opened in 1879.

At that time the building comprised of a ground floor containing the police court with a clerk s office and a retiring room.

The floor above had more offices for the Council and the staff.

Picture of the
Loftus Town Hall
taken in 2009
by the author.

There is no record of any petty sessions in the 1845 return, but a Loftus Bench certainly existed in later years, as is evidenced by the above remarks and description of the Town Hall premises, and the fact that it shared a clerk with Guisborough, Redcar and South Bank and it probably dealt with cases in part of Langbaurgh East.

Nevertheless it became the victim of rationalisation and although no date has been put upon the change, Si n Jones considers that it probably merged in with Guisborough at some earlier stage, or certainly by the 1968 rationalisation as seems to be the case when reading Malcolm Race s publication.

In 2009, as it has been so for many years, this fine Town Hall is the seat of the local Town Council.

On the author s visit in 2009, a casual conversation with an interested passing citizen, who turned out to be a Town Councillor, provided some pert observations on governance of townships in these times.

Redcar

The town was part of the North Riding but in 1968 the town became part of the County Borough of Teesside. It is now within the ceremonial county of North Yorkshire as Redcar and Cleveland.

A court was held from 1910 as a part of the East Langbaurgh PSD, to serve the coastal towns. It had a courtroom attached to the Police Station on Church Lane, but it was not until the turn of the 20th century that a separate court for the town had been considered.

Via Malcolm Race s publication reference is made to a history of Redcar and Coatham by Janet Cockroft that the Redcar Council first raised the matter of a local court in 1901, but this move lay fallow as at that time the Guisborough justices did not consider there to be enough business in the town to justify a court.

It was not until 1905 when a gathering of Guisborough justices heard an appeal from a magistrate that a court should be opened to deal with cases in Redcar and other nearby parishes.

The motion was approved but it was not an immediate item for action, and it was to be 1909 before magistrates met in Redcar to examine the newly built (1908) police station.

The 1908 police station.

Picture provided by courtesy of
St John Pilkington
taken in 2009 .

From then it was decided to build a courthouse as an addition to the police station. That opened for business on 21st January 1910.

St John Pilkington took this picture in 2009, and the author is grateful for his kind permission to reproduce it here. The evidence is that the magistrates would have a problem parking these days.

This bench served, sitting weekly on Fridays, until the first rationalisations in 1968. The police station and courtroom survived, the latter seemingly converted to residential use. In 2009 the police station appeared to be scheduled for another fate.

As earlier noted the Clerk to the court was multi tasked with others in the area, and shortly before the 1968 rationalisation was covering courts in Stokesley as well as those far away at Richmond and Northallerton.

Malcolm Race in his booklet, page 32, suggests that in 1968 some of the cases from the closed Redcar court were taken at Loftus or Guisborough until all were eventually only taken at that latter town or Middlesbrough, as is now the case.

We then move on to the fast growing Victorian and Edwardian seaside town of Saltburn, founded in 1861. There seems to be a query as to whether the magistrates ever sat in the town; there being some impression that there might have been occasions when cases would have been taken in a room at the police station or the local town offices, but no firm evidence has been provided to substantiate this. This may have arisen as one reference to Saltburn on the internet turns up some information on Redcar, and a failure to read the title could confuse.

No-one within present memory can recall such, and those venturing an opinion going back to the 1960s, say that all cases were taken at Redcar, the division being Redcar and Saltburn.

Yarm and Thornaby

The town of Yarm seems to have arisen as a result of it being the crossing point over the river Tees at the top end of the tidal flow, a bridge having been built there in earlier years, and replaced by more modern structures in more recent times.

It had at one time covered part of the area which is now within Middlesbrough but in the late 1800s, as the latter town grew in status, Yarm declined.

Nevertheless, Yarm was blessed with a fine Town Hall which was built in 1710 by the Lord of the Manor, a gentleman by name of Thomas Belasyse. No doubt the premises were constructed as were so many others of traditional moot hall fashion, with a court on the first floor and opportunities for traders beneath.

The 1845 petty sessional return mentions the court sitting in a room called the Town s Hall belonging to the lord of the manor, noting that the premises were rent free but a small sum was paid by the clerk to the local bailiff for preparing the room.

An interesting combination of pictures tells the story of the opening and a later 18th century event.

Pictures by Geoff Smith.

Si n Jones writes to the author, that the courthouse in the Town Square, which features in many pictures of Yarm, now houses a public toilet. One assumes that this is only a small part of current usage and that other parts maintain a suitable dignity.

In *Six into One will Go* it is mentioned how both Yarm and Thornaby courts were closely linked with those of Stockton-on-Tees in County Durham. It is remarked that as Thornaby grew because of its proximity to Stockton the work reduced in Yarm and the courts were transferred from Yarm to being wholly held at Thornaby by the late 19th century, in a court room attached to the police station on George Street, and this continued to be the case until the changes in 1968. Thornaby closed first and then on January 26th 1973 was the last sitting of magistrates in Stockton.

A view of the Thornaby courthouse is shown at the end of this section. This is also etched into a glass screen at the Middlesbrough courthouse.

One delightful *vignette* of circumstances is contributed in *Six into One will Go'* by retired magistrate, Mrs Margaret Holt of Yarm. When she first sat in 1962 at Thornaby she recalls .

"At first we used to have one court a week and we went along once a fortnight sitting seven to a bench. When it became busier we began to hold two courts simultaneously - and our retiring room was used to accommodate the people waiting to appear because there was nowhere else for them to go". ...and then she adds.....

"If we had to adjourn for lunch, we went into the police station next door and one of the police officers would go across to a transport café and bring us back delicious sandwiches – which we ate in the station. I wonder what would be said about that now?"

It is fair enough to say that times have changed , as such intimacy with the Force would be greatly frowned upon these days.

South Bank

South Bank was originally a small town within the former urban area of Middlesbrough, lying towards the mouth of the Tees and obviously on the south side. It is a now a ward within the borough of Redcar and Cleveland lying within the ceremonial county of North Yorkshire. In the 19th century, as with Middlesbrough the town grew, at least industrially, with huge dockyards and ancillary works.

Si n Jones considers th at the court might have been formed at a similar time to the Middlesbrough bench in 1857, but this has yet to be verified. There is no note of any court being held in the 1845 sessional return.

The court was a section of Langbaurgh North as an offshoot from Stockton on Tees. As with so many other smaller courts, the premises were attached to the police station and were previously known as police courts. At times the premises were inadequate to take the number of cases and offices across the street had to be used. In 2009 St John Pilkington reports that the buildings are demolished.

The South Bank Courthouse, attached to the Police Station, closed in 1973 when it, with Stockton Court, merged with Middlesbrough in the Teesside Law Courts in Victoria Square.

The South Bank Courthouse, attached to Police Station.
Picture by kind courtesy of Malcolm Race JP.

Middlesbrough

In 1968 the County Borough of Teesside was established, and the town of Middlesbrough, which had been part of the North Riding of Yorkshire since its inception, was made centre of the administrally inspired new county borough. Further boundary changes in 1974 established the county of Cleveland, incorporating the new borough.

The arrangement was never comfortable, as the traditional links with Yorkshire which had been developed over generations, haunted the new arrangement. In 1996, the boundary manipulators decided to ditch Cleveland as a failure, making Middlesbrough into a unitary authority within the ceremonial county of North Yorkshire. So somewhat battered and bruised this wandering member of the Yorkshire family more or less returned home.

From a court point of view, the name Teesside stuck, and that is the name which covers the magisterial work now being carried out at the Middlesbrough Courthouse. As will have been noted from the foregoing, with the exception of Guisborough, all the other six courts south of the Tees have been merged into the one building, hence the title of Malcolm Race s booklet, *Six into one will go,* but let the reader decide whether that expression was one of administrative frustration or magisterial acceptance of the inevitable.

Of course, other benches from north of the Tees have been brought into the modern bench, but for the purposes of this exercise it will concentrate on the incorporation of those from Yorkshire.

The development of the present Teesside magistrates courts in Middlesbrough has not been a simple one, despite its relatively short life. In the first place, some of the Langbaurgh North justices had been meeting in the town at premises in Graham Street, but in 1860 had then moved to the Station Hotel on Station Street, where a room was made available at the rear.

The first Commission of the Peace for Middlesbrough itself was granted in July 1855, only two years after the town received its Charter of Incorporation, then two years later in January 1857 the first petty sessional court was held in Middlesbrough. However, that was not a simple matter as until there was a place provided in the town the defendants had to go to Yarm or Stokesley for their case to be taken; hardly an auspicious beginning.

That was resolved for the time being in 1889, when the Municipal Buildings were opened, and a magnificent courtroom was to do justice to the proceedings for some of the next 84 years.

The imposing building, showing its key position in the borough in 2009 with foreground activities.

There are now no courts held therein.

The Town Hall.
Picture by courtesy of Roger Robinson.

Well before then it had been getting increasingly difficult to work in the premises, as it was affected by Quarter Sessions as they came around, quite apart from the growing inadequacy of the offices and other facilities. In his book, Malcolm Race notes these problems and there is interesting comment on the work in those years.

Of course, this was not uncommon throughout the county as the Town Halls met with the same problem of increasing work loads in administration as well as dispensing local justice.

In 1973 the Teesside Law courts were opened, having been built on the site of a demolished school in Victoria Square and they took the strain. In the building there were six magistrates courts, five Crown Courts and a juvenile court, a rare bird for those days, but which prevented the previous necessity of closing off courtrooms for that specific purpose.

An interesting by-product of this new building venture was that later in 1977 the embryo future Cleveland Council was able to meet in a courtroom.

There was yet a further change, as in 1992, when a new Combined Court Centre was opened to take the Crown and County Courts, the magistrates were able to open their wings into the former Crown Court rooms in the 1973 premises, and that is the position as at the moment when this piece was compiled in 2009.

Teesside Magistrates Courts in 2009.
Picture taken and produced here by courtesy of Roger Robinson.

During the years, as will have been gathered from the other short articles preceding this, various other pieces of the adjacent PSDs have been taken into the Teesside Courts, Guisborough now being the only home for magisterial justice in that area of the Ceremonial County of North Yorkshire outside Middlesbrough, next stop being Scarborough or Northallerton.

However, it is rather nice that these other venues which served justice in the area have been commemorated in the modern building by decorative etched glass screens in the area of the main entrance, and a couple of examples are shown overleaf. Some difficulty to avoid background reflections when taking photographs still allows the quality of the etchings to be seen, and they present a useful historic pictorial link with those earlier seats of justice.

Glass etching of Thornaby Courthouse.
Picture by courtesy of Roger Robinson.

Glass etching of South Bank Courthouse.
Picture by courtesy of Roger Robinson.

FOUR

EAST YORKSHIRE

The 1974 Boundary Review saw the old East Riding being put into an amorphous mass known as the County of Humberside which extended into parts of Lindsey, North Lincolnshire, to make one new county. Of all the country wide manipulations by the faceless powers in Whitehall, this one was doomed from the start.

The Members of Parliament and citizens generally within this ill-matched combination fought against the bureaucracy which had brought it about, and in 1996 it was broken up, allowing the section north of the Humber Estuary to be reinstated with its proud title, East Riding of Yorkshire. Broadly speaking, geographically it now remains much as it was before the tinkering.

The wapentakes numbered 12, divided as follows

Ouse & Derwent. To the South East of York, East of Selby.

Harthill Wilton Beacon. East of the above.

Buckrose. North East of the above, East of York.

Dickering. East of Buckrose to the coast at Bridlington etc.

Harthill Holme Beacon. South of Wilton Beacon.

Howdenshire.

Harthill Hunsley Beacon. Around and North of Beverley.

Harthill Bainton Beacon. North of the above.

Holderness North. Towards Hornsea on the coast.

Holderness Middle.

Holderness South. Coastal, Withernsea towards Spurn Point.

Kingston-upon-Hull.

The main exceptions to the historical former East Riding are the exclusion of Norton, now taken into North Yorkshire, and the inclusion of Goole which formerly was in the old West Riding. There was a court held at Escrick in the Ouse and Derwent Division, but latterly this moved into York prior to being joined with the Selby PSD, now part of North Yorkshire.

Within the Riding there was always a clear division between the lower lying coastal divisions of Holderness and the Wolds areas further inland and to the North. That remains so to this day as the areas of Holderness are administered with Hull in a composite unit under the aegis of the main office in Beverley.

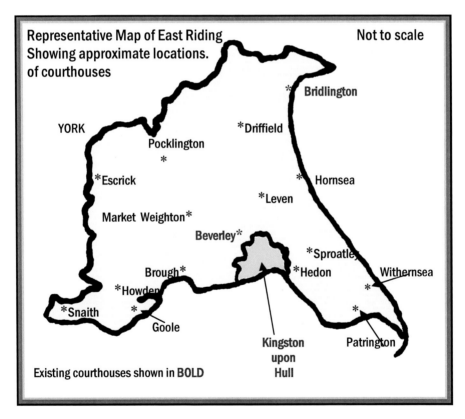

At Bainton near Driffield sessions are mentioned in the 1845 Return of Petty Sessions, which were taken in The New Inn.

It is also recorded in the 1845 return that sessions for South Hunsley Beacon were held in Hessle at a room in the Poor House . Certainly in other places there are references to a lock-up in Hessle and at Welton, however, in respect of the former, present day local historians are unaware of those happenings or the venue.

More specifically, the following notes whilst taking us back in time where information is available, largely refer to the various venues which continued into the 20th century and were closed in the years thereafter, even up to the period bridging the next millennium change.

Amongst providers of information. Martin Craven of Hessle has been of great assistance with his depth of knowledge, and Neil Marquis, lately of the East Riding Courts staff, has provided many of the pictures and much assistance with further information; he also hosted a most useful visit by the author to Goole courthouse.

Escrick

Situated on the A19 South of York on the very edge of the riding, Escrick sittings of magistrates are described in the records of the East Riding at the Treasure House Beverley as

"Petty Sessions (for Ouse and Derwent Wapentake) are held monthly in the Court Room at the Police Station". [T.Bulmer, *History and Directory of East Yorkshire*, 1892, p. 607.]

In *Escrick: A Village History*, author J.P.G. Taylor writes in 1999 .. *"Did the existence of a police station in the village with a resident inspector have a deterrent effect on prospective malefactors? This was the large imposing building in an austere classical style which had been put up on the Skipwith road in 1857-58. ..... The police station incorporated a court room and here the magistrates met in petty sessions once a month to dispense justice. Lord Wenlock, of course, was a magistrate, chairman, in fact, of the Ouse and Derwent Division. The building is now divided into flats".*

However, even before then, the 1845 return of sessions made to Parliament tells us in that year the courts were held in public houses; there being a choice of three in Riccall, The Drovers Inn, The Hare and Hounds, and The Greyhound Inn. Escrick had more modest demands with one venue at The Spotted Bull Inn, The busy chap who clerked these petty sessions and possibly tasted the various tavern brews after each, was Charles Newstead of Selby.

Michael Rawnsley, lately Clerk to the Justices in York and the Western Clerkship of North Yorkshire, has been most helpful in providing a considerable amount of information and his comments to the author include

Regarding Escrick - I can recall clearly seeing some licensing plans for approval dated the 1930s, the approval of which took place at the Escrick Courthouse. I suspect, at the local police station because of course before the Magistrates Courts Act 1952 all courts were hitherto known as Police Courts. Escrick would be part of Ouse and Derwent and within the (old) East Riding. When I came to

York in 1971 Ouse and Derwent sat at the Castle in York (then the Quarter Sessions/Assize) court building prior to the creation of the Crown Court system on 1ˢᵗ January1972 - they 'borrowed' a room for their twice monthly Monday afternoon sittings. Escrick then went into the (new) Selby PSD on 1.4.74".

The former Escrick Police Station and Courthouse.

Picture kindly taken and provided by J P G Taylor

Plainly the magistrates sitting at Escrick must have moved into York some time before 1971, the court room then being returned to the police.

In 2009 the building is a rather nice block of apartments.

I am grateful to J P G Taylor and Michael Rawnsley for their contributions to this piece.

Brough

An interesting article in the East Riding Journal of November 9th 2009 tells us that Brough can trace its history back further than most, to when it was known as Petuaria during the Roman period and served as the capital of the Celtic tribe of the Parisi. It was first a Roman fort, founded in 70 AD and abandoned in about 125.

It was at the southern end of the Roman road known as Cade s Road, which ran for a hundred miles via York to what is now known as Newcastle-upon-Tyne.

Some 20th century excavations discovered a dedication stone of a Roman theatre which is unusual as also being the only recorded written mention of a magistrate in Roman Britain.

The Ferry Inn on Station Road is famous as having been a place which allegedly gave hospitality to Dick Turpin.

The Brough Courthouse.
Photograph by courtesy of Neil Marquis.

Brough courthouse which was built in 1911-1912 was also incorporated with the police station. The whole cost of both premises was noted as £2,000.

When Howden Court closed in 1995, the work first came to Brough but all cases finally moved away in 1998, when the Goole & Howdenshire Division was established. Brough then closed as a courthouse.

However, during the period of change when courts were being merged into Beverley and with the changeover of courthouses in that town from old to new, some of the sittings were temporarily moved to Brough, but after then in 2001 the court was closed permanently, thus ending nearly 2,000 years of local justice.

Welton

The 1845 Return of Petty Sessions advises that the sittings for South Hunsley Beacon were held weekly in the Blacksmith s Arms at Riplingham. The inn is no more. Concerning Welton, files at the East Riding Treasure House in Beverley mention that in 1913 there was a contract for alterations to the old police station/courthouse, originally built in 1850. Martin Craven, the local historian, comments that he has noted that cases for South Hunsley Beacon were held there and this is confirmed in the notes associated with Richard Pearson s picture of the Police Station in his book of sketches.

However, Kelly s Directory of 1893 is more explicit, making reference that Petty Sessions for that division were held in Hull at the Town Hall every Tuesday at 1030am and at Welton every alternate Monday, also at 1030am. Kelly augments this information with a list of twenty one magistrates in the division, there being two chairmen, one for the division and one for the Hull bench; the Clerk being Mr J Parke Chatham of Bowlalley Lane in Hull.

Martin Craven and the author visited Welton on a rather indifferent day in February 2010 and the following picture shows the premises.

Welton Police Station.

Author's picture.

Howden

In 1845, for the sum of £2.12s, the petty sessions were held in the Half Moon Inn, so said George England the Clerk in his Return to Parliament.

By 1900 cases were held in the combined police and court building shown below. These were on Bridgegate in the style of others designed by Alfred Beaumont, and they were opened in 1900.

The Howden Courthouse and Police Station.

Photograph by courtesy of Neil Marquis.

Howden Magistrates Court closed in 1995 and the work went to Brough until 1998 when the cases were transferred to the Goole Courthouse as the Goole & Howdenshire Division was formed.

The premises have now been replaced with the offices of the Press Association Operations Centre. 2003 saw the completion of their building on the site of the old courthouse and police station. The modern world has certainly come to historic Howden.

Goole

Originally being just about the most easterly major town in the former West Riding, Goole has played an important part in the life of Yorkshire. From its former use as a convenient trading post for the Dutch, the development of the coalfields and the linkage by river and canal to the heartland of industrial West Yorkshire towns and cities, as well as south via the Trent, it became a town of great significance.

Apart from earliest times, in the 19th century one place where justice was applied was the Gaol House. The building survives as a lively public house but with the modernised version of the name emblazoned on the premises.

There is no attractive view with all the additions of promotional advertising.

Originally, it must have been quite a handsome building.

Author's pictures.

Presumably, as with other like premises, the accommodation would house the constabulary as well as provide a court room for use by the justices.

The major change came in 1888 when the new premises shown below were built to house both the police and the courts. The size of the development alone signifies the importance of Goole, as it will have been noticed that the premises built in other towns about this time were rather more modest.

Goole Police Station and Courthouse, built in 1888 still in use in 2009.
Picture by courtesy of Neil Marquis.

These premises were opened on Friday March 9th 1888 with a considerable degree of legal pride and general jollification. Speeches were made by everyone from the Chairman of the Bench, the Clerk, the Police and the Solicitors, before taking the cases for the day.

The latter can not have taken over long, as the programme, overleaf, has the firm notice at the end - LUNCH 2pm.

The Goole courthouse, together with adjacent police station, in 2009 continued to serve the community in this part of the Lower Osgoldcross Division based on the original wapentake.

Programme for the opening of the Goole Courthouse in 1888.

Author's picture.

Chairman T W Yew 1893 (above). To the left a view of the main court room in 2009.

Pictures taken by the author, by kind permission of Neil Marquis, May 2009.

In 2010 it has been decided that it will no longer serve the community, as it is to be closed under the government savings needs interpreted by the administration. With the closure of Selby that will mean no courthouse directly between Leeds and Beverley or Hull.

Great Driffield

The Petty Sessional Division of Bainton Beacon in the Saxon wapentake of Harthill was centred on the Driffield villages, of which the larger of the two became the town which eventually assumed the seat of office for the local courts. There is mention of The Old Town Hall, Bell Hotel, Market Place, but the author has not discovered if courts were ever held there. Baines in 1823 makes no mention of them but notes that Mr John Lamplugh, a sheriff's officer, lived on Bridge Street.

For some time the courts for the PSD also sat in The New Inn at Bainton, such being recorded in the 1845 Return of Petty Sessions.

A Mechanics Institute was established in Driffield in 1837 but it was not until 1856 when new premises were built in Exchange Street by a Mr E D Conyers, and these were used for magisterial and county court purposes.

It would therefore seem that the premises listed in the 1845 Great Driffield return of Petty Sessions as public rooms would be the temporary Mechanics Institute, but it is interesting to note that the Clerk making the return was an Eden D Conyers, of Driffield, and that a fee of *'2£(sic) per year'* was paid to the trustees of the rooms.

Driffield Mechanics Institute Building in 2009.
Picture by kind permission of Mr John Harrison FRICS FAAV.

In 1843 a new police station for the Division was erected on Eastgate North in Great Driffield, and this housed a total of eleven constables with their sergeant, a house being included in the premises for the superintendent to be accommodated. There was no provision for magistrates so the sessions continued in the Mechanics Institute.

These premises continued to be used for the next half century plus, but there were increasing concerns that the premises had no courtroom attached, and that was considered desirable in those days.

After searching the town for an appropriate site a new police station with a courthouse was built on Wansford Road in 1897. The premises were comprehensively fitted out with courtrooms as well as magistrates rooms and county court rooms. This then served the community until the courts section was closed under further reforms of 2001. The police continued to use the premises, but the cases and the courts transferred to Beverley.

I am indebted to Mr Wally Simpkin, a local historian, for his input of information.

The Police Station and Court House on Wansford Road.
Photograph by courtesy of Neil Marquis.

Market Weighton

The Petty Sessions for the district were held in a room at the Police Station which had been built in 1843 and which stood on The Green.

THE OLD POLICE STATION ON THE GREEN, MARKET WEIGHTON

Picture by courtesy of Enid Greenwood.

Enid Greenwood, a retired magistrate, has been kind enough to allow me to comment from her book *Market Weighton, Changing Face and Faces* which she published in 2000.

In this she recalls that the local newspaper had reported on a meeting in 1901 when the state of the premises was much criticised by the justices. It was extremely damp and not good for the health of the magistrates or the prisoners.

There was a considerable debate in which it was suggested that as a new courthouse had been built in Pocklington it would be cheaper to allow the Market Weighton justices to meet there.

This was not felt to be satisfactory and there was much pressure applied to make sure that justice continued to be meted out in Market Weighton. Local feelings won the day over red tape and parsimony and in 1903 a new building for police and magistrates was opened on the Beverley Road. This is shown overleaf.

The Courthouse and Police Station.
Another of Alfred Beaumont's designs.
Photograph by courtesy of Neil Marquis.

This courthouse on Beverley Road continued to be used for sessions, albeit at times it was not overfull with offenders. In fact there is a record that in 1917, there being no cases for the session, the presiding justice, Mr T G Lyon, was presented with a pair of white gloves, not an over regular occurrence anywhere.

The amount of business was a factor when in 1995 it was eventually decided that Market Weighton cases could be moved to Pocklington and so that took place. To be fair, the record showing 99 hours of sittings in one year made Market Weighton one of the least busy in the county.

Thus Market Weighton lost its seat of justice and nowadays the cases will all be heard at Beverley in the modern courthouse.

Pocklington

Baines is silent on justice in 1823, but the 1845 Return of Petty Sessions gives the venue as the lock-up house ; stating *"there is a large room attached to the lock-up house, in which the petty and special sessions are held".*

Other records show that in 1856 a Police Station was used for the session of the Wilton Beacon Division in the Harthill wapentake.

Bulmer s *History and Directory of East Yorkshire 1892* states in that year the Petty Sessions were held in the Magistrates Room, on Great George Street.

The East Riding Archives record that a new courthouse and a police station with superintendent s house were built on George Street in 1898. Despite the addition of Market Weighton business in 1995, when the courthouse was improved to a decent standard, the work load was small and plans were made to amalgamate with others in the district. The courthouse continued to be used until the last sitting was held there in 2001.

The last Courthouse on George Street, Pocklington.
Photograph by courtesy of Neil Marquis.

However, to add to that basic outline I am greatly obliged to Andrew Sefton, archivist of Pocklington and District Local History Group, as result of which there is rather more to add to this particular tale of the town s seats of justice, drawing attention to the following.

In earlier times there were the customary manor courts and in Pocklington the town was divided with that of the Dean of York at one end of the town and the Dolman family at the other. Later these leet courts became manor courts under the Lord of the Manor who in this case was the head of the Duncombe family of Kilnwick Percy.

This information is drawn from David Neave s publication *Pocklington 1660-1914*, as is the information that in about 1847 a superintendent of police was appointed and a court house was built.

However, prior to then, according to Neave, there had been in former years a market hall and court room of medieval vintage, but that had fallen into a sad state by the end of the 17th century.

There were county courts held in the Oddfellows Hall, which was on Union Street, in the 19th century. In that same period reference is made in directories to the Magistrates Room and court held six times a year on Great George Street, round about the same time the police house and station, noted above, were built.

From all the above it seems to be fairly certain that premises on George Street featured as the venue for magistrates courts from the 19th century until closure in 2001 when the cases, together with those previously transferred from Market Weighton, were sent to the new courthouse in Beverley.

Thus, as with so many other smaller towns, an interesting slice of history in Pocklington came to an end.

Beverley

In the 19th century Beverley had two courts, a borough court held in the Guildhall and the East Riding Sessions House for the rest of the Riding. Petty sessions, held at the Guildhall, could be on more than one day in the week. In either instance the most serious crimes, such as any attracting capital punishment, were tried in York.

Beverley Guildhall.
Picture kindly provided by Neil Marquis.

The Guildhall is marked as being an 18th century building, but in fact the Guildhall premises site dates from before the 15th century. Indeed a building on the site was purchased even earlier in 1501.

One part of the site continued to house the Guildhall, but a Sessions House was also constructed, together with the House of Correction, both of the latter surviving until the 17th century, when a charity school was sited in the latter location. Then some time later, towards the end of the 18th century, a prison and police station were constructed there.

There is an entry in the 1845 Return of Petty Sessions for the Guildhall and Courthouse being the venues for sessions for the borough.

Those recorded as being held in the Sessions House were for the East Riding Division of North Hunsley Beacon. It seems that the mixture of crimes committed in and around Beverley was much as elsewhere in the Riding, although a tendency to drunkenness was notable, especially on Market day.

The Sessions House building, as it is today, was built in the period 1805-1810, the architect being Charles Watson of Wakefield, and it shows similar grandeur of other imposing courthouses of the time, such as the Sessions House at Pontefract which was designed by the same architect. Petty Sessions were recorded here in the 1845 return to Parliament which mentioned the premises as being next to the Gaol . This would be the East Riding House of Correction which was by then established as a custody centre and workhouse for those who had been sentenced, of which more is said below.

The Sessions House, now a Spa, together with the House of Correction were set adjacent to each other, on North Bar Without, on the road approaching the town from Driffield.

The Sessions House, Beverley.
Author's picture 2010.

An interesting point is that the Sessions House neighbour, the House of Correction, provided education and work for the prisoners. The work included turning a treadmill which ground up chalk which was used for manufacturing whiting. This was no doubt used by the local paint manufacturing business in the town and others in Hull nearby. The House of Correction opened in 1810 and closed in 1878 when it was converted into a house.

After the 1974 local government boundary changes, cases for the Borough and adjacent parts of the Riding were combined into the Guildhall.

A new Beverley Courthouse, opened in 2001, is situated on Champney Road and this now houses all the southern half of the East Riding County magistrates court work, other than that of the City of Hull and the Holderness divisions which have been taken into Hull.

Beverley Magistrates Courts.
Author's picture 2010.

Bridlington

As with other ancient places, the Courts were often associated with places of worship, York and Selby being two notable examples. Likewise was Bridlington.

A 14th century construction, The Bayle was the entrance to the original Priory. It variously housed a prison, a school, a religious assembly room, a Court room, a garrison, and then a Town Hall. As a Court the room extended across the whole of the upper floor, a very impressive space indeed.

The Bayle, Bridlington Priory.
Picture by the author in 2010.

Baines Directory for 1823 is silent on the matter of the courts and justices in Bridlington, other than a reference to a large room above the arch not far from the West End of the old Priory church, which was used partly as a *Town's Hall* and as a National School. This appears to be a description of the same premises. The room was above the Kit cote which were rather gloomy cells used for the containment of petty offenders.

However, by the 19th century venues had changed and other premises in what is now called the Old Town were in use.

I am obliged to John S Walker of Bridlington for some very interesting information about court matters in that town. He writes to me .

"In the 1960's I was allowed to clear Lamberts solicitor's office archive at no 70 High Street. At the rear of the property was a magistrates court (up the yard at the side known as Cranswick's yard). Sadly I didn't take any photographs, but I was looking at a very early court, witness box, jury benches etc., and from subsequent research I rather think that this was very much reminiscent of a Georgian court."

"I rescued many important documents, the one that is relevant to your enquiry was an early court book which I handed to the library at Kingst (sic) for safe keeping. Whether it is still there I haven't had time to ascertain. The property in Cranswick's yard has recently been refurbished, so any trace of its original use has gone."

The door to the left of the bay windows would be the entrance to Cranswick s Yard.

**70 High Street is the white building.
In 2010 it is a hairdresser's.**
Author's picture in 2010.

He continues ..   *"Rev Dr Purvis did much local research (he set up the Borthwick institute in York). I inherited through the*

Augustinian society of Bridlington, many pictures and research documents,.........

.........one picture that sticks in my mind is of the ancient courthouse on Squire Lane. The building has long gone".

Squire Lane as it is in 2010 when pictured by the author. The yard behind is as bare as the alleyway.

As yet the period when these various premises were used is not clear, but it could be that in Cranswick s Yard was the forerunner of the one shown below which was built in 1881.

Incorporated in a Police Station, the former Courthouse on Quay Road was built in 1881. Designed by Smith & Brodrick it cost £4,000.
Photograph by courtesy of Neil Marquis.

The Black Lion Inn.
Author's picture 2010.

What we do know for certain is that the Dickering justices are recorded in 1845 as sitting in the Black Lion Inn, the events being testified by Mr Sidney Taylor.

The Return also notes that unlike many landlords who were satisfied with the business brought to the custom of the house , in this case a rent was paid to Mr George Nicholson, the Landlord.

Ultimately, later in the 20th century, the 1881 premises shown on the previous page were closed for court purposes, although they were retained by the police

and the new courthouse on Quay Road became the home for the magistrates.

The Present Courthouse.
Picture by the author 2010.

Holderness

The area to the East of Kingston-upon-Hull, although it is in the East Riding of Yorkshire, has an identity of its own. The ancient wapentake of Holderness from which it is contrived was divided into three, North, Middle and South.

It would not be unfair to comment that the area is not widely known to the general population of the country, even amongst many residents of Yorkshire. The main attractions of the east coast to the industrial west of the county have been to the more commercial high-lights further north; the softer areas of the Holderness plain and its noted bird populations have drawn those seeking a quieter break. The coastal resort of Withernsea has always retained an air which has appealed to the less noisy holiday makers.

The major town with an ancient historical base is Hedon and there are numerous other villages in this delightful area of country on the peninsular leading to Spurn Point.

Right at the top is the town of Hornsea, which is notably further north and nearer to Bridlington, almost within the wider East Riding. The latter town benefited largely when Hornsea court was closed.

The other courthouses which have been used in more recent times, up to the latest closures when all work was telescoped down to Hull, were at
 Hedon,
 Patrington,
 Withernsea,
 Leven,
 Sproatley

Martin Craven has greatly assisted in the researches into this area and accompanied the author and his wife on a very enlightening trip in the Spring of 2009.

Hornsea

The 1845 Returns showed Leven as the seat for the North Holderness Petty Sessions. Courts were not held in Hornsea until 1923 when they were held at the Public Rooms in Newbegin. In 1927, they moved to the U.D.C offices in Cliff Road Elim Lodge . They remained there until 1973 when the courts went to Parva Road.

Martin Lonsdale, a magistrate in the town at the time, recalls that when he first sat as a justice the petty sessions were held in the Council Chamber of the former UDC at Elim Lodge on Cliff Road. This was a room which had been built on to a Victorian house.

This picture of Elim Lodge was taken by his grandfather and seems to show an extension to the left of the main building.

However on this modern picture to the right the extension is plainly very different and Martin Lonsdale, who provided both of these pictures, says   .

……..."Elim Lodge became the HQ of Hornsea UDC, I think, before WW1 and the white building on the left became the council chamber. This was used by the North Holderness Justices until 1973. It was very inconvenient for the Police at Hornsea as the station was nearly a

mile away and there was nowhere to hold prisoners. We used to retire into the sitting room of the resident caretaker which was hired every other Wednesday".

What is known was that the Council Chamber was scarcely adequate and generally the facilities were not satisfactory for modern justice to be dispensed in an appropriate way.

On opening new premises in December 1973, they were hailed by Lord Halifax as being very well equipped for dealing with justice in the 20th century.

Situated on the sea front between Parva Road and Railway Street, the courthouse was provided in 1973, being linked to the Police Station.

The Courthouse at Hornsea.
Picture by courtesy of Neil Marquis.

The magistrates from Leven had previously transferred to Hornsea and it was there that justice continued to be dispensed until the next round of changes which took place, culminating in the closure of Hornsea courthouse in 2001.

Casework went to Bridlington, but former Leven area work went to Beverley when the new Bridlington Courthouse was built.

Hedon

The ancient borough of Hedon dates from its foundation in 1130 and the first charter granted by Royal Charter in 1158 which raised it in the rank of privileges with York and Lincoln. It was the major port on the north side of the Humber estuary, and remained so until the industrial revolution caused the upstart next door neighbour, hitherto a modest village, to be developed in more recent times.

The courts of the burgesses were first held in 1348 as a result of a Royal Charter from Edward III; a Mayor and bailiffs being those responsible for the law, within the boundaries of the borough, under the terms of the charter. From 1692, when the Town Hall was built, courts were held therein, although for a short period circa 1742 the courts appear to have taken place in the New Hall in Fletchergate.

Hedon Town Hall.
Picture taken by the author in 2009.

Except for Hull and Sculcoates, the other courthouses were all part of a rash of similar buildings across the East Riding where a courtroom was an adjunct of the police station. These sprouted up as a result of The Municipal Corporations Act of 1835. However, in Hedon things carried on as before until the passing of the Hedon Corporation and Borough Improvement Act of 1860.

The new regulations for the borough, whilst strengthening the body corporate of the town, removed the magisterial duties to the East Riding of the County of York. As a temporary expedient only the former mayor and the incumbent in that office were allowed to stay as magistrates. Petty Sessions ceased to be held in Hedon in 1872 on transfer to the Sproatley courthouse.

As with many other ancient boroughs in the country, the 1972 Act of Parliament which brought about boundary changes on 1st April 1974 reduced the borough in present day terms, although it could not take away the proud traditions of its past.

This picture on the left shows the former courtroom, although the additional table and chairs in the foreground are an extra for council committees.

The picture to the right is of the Coat of Arms which on the picture above is merely a dark rectangle on the upper part of the wall over the Bench.

Both these pictures were taken by the author in 2009.

The Court Room and the rooms adjacent were of course used as the Council Chamber for the former Hedon Borough Council, and they continue to be used by the present Town Council.

The picture to the right is of the room which would have been used as a retiring room for the justices.

Picture by the author.

It now houses interesting pictures and records of former times and still acts as a retiring room for the Mayor of the Town Council.

The Town Hall is still active with the work of the Hedon Town Council which sits in what was also the court room of the ancient borough, all as pictured on the previous page.

Magistrates from Hedon who moved to Sproatley no longer sit there, the courts having been translated with all the others from Holderness into Hull.

Sproatley

Sproatley is central to the Middle Holderness Division and in 1849 a Police Station and Court House were erected, and in the latter the petty sessions were held.

Sproatley Police Station and Courthouse.
Author's picture.

This picture shows it in 2009 after much hard work put in by the owners Mark and Sandra Betts who kindly gave their permission for the author to take and use the pictures in this piece.

However, prior to the site for the above fine building being provided by the authorities on land given by the late Sir Clifford-Constable in 1849, it is on record that in 1845 cases for Middle Holderness were taken in the Public Hall in Sculcoates a room therein being granted free to the justices. The clerk submitting the record to Parliament was Mr Charles Fox of Hull. Of course it is more than likely that many cases would be taken in Hedon, just down the road and also in Middle Holderness.

After the Sproatley premises were built the court sessions were held monthly.

Since those earlier days when the courthouse was built some additions have been made, not the least in the most recent changes, but it is nice to be able to record on these pages how the building was in its policing and magisterial hey-day, and the pictures below give some idea of those times. The first of these shows the premises as a whole from the same angle as the modern view.

All the pictures on this page shown by courtesy of Mark & Sandra Betts.

The above picture has some slight distortion but clearly shows the limit of the building although the accommodation inside was remarkably generous by comparison with many others of these dual purpose buildings.

This cell was one of two, this being for males, the other cell was for women. A solid wood bunk bed is low right.

The imposing front door shows the sign Police Station. In those days courts were named Police Courts.

In 1964 there were some alterations and improvements made to bring the premises up to required standards for current times.

The court sat on alternate Wednesdays.

Paul Willmer, a Legal Team Manager in Hull in 2009, recalls from his earlier days when taking courts, that should the sittings go past lunch time, all parties would adjourn to the Blue Bell public house nearby, where they took up traditional places in various parts of the building. Furthermore he recalls an ink blotter on the desk having a calendar left with the dates in 1945 around VE Day.

The premises continued to be used by the justices for hearing cases until 1995 when they were closed on all the court s business being transferred to Hull.

By courtesy of the Dalesman and its very helpful editor, Paul Jackson, this author is pleased to be able to include a letter from the November 2010 edition of that journal, written by John Q Smith of Knaresborough.

"The article 'Rough Justice' by Martin Limon (August) was yet another contribution to bring on a wave of nostalgia, as my brother-in-law was Sproatley's village policeman in the mid 1960s. Ron Hunter and my sister Joan lived in the police house adjoining the court. I recollect Ron arriving home early for his dinner saying that a prisoner at Hull gaol had escaped "I'll just have a bit to eat and then I'll pick him up," he said. "Just like that?" I retorted.

Ron returned later. "Did you arrest him, then?" I asked.

"Yes, he's on his way back now".

To Ron this was routine as prisoners escaping Hull Prison often headed for the bus station and caught the bus to Preston, not knowing that Preston of course is a Holderness village just south of Sproatley."

Such gems add to the rich culture of what has, over centuries, been the backbone of the local justice system in England.

Withernsea

As a main town in South Holderness, Withernsea had a court house designed in 1898 and it is recorded that by 1901 Petty Sessions were being held in that Court House on Railway Crescent.

Withernsea Courthouse and Police Station.
By courtesy of Clark Weightman & Co.

This above combination of pictures, kindly provided by Carl Bradley of Clark Weightman & Co, Chartered Surveyors of Hessle who had the premises to sell in 2009, of the complex at Withernsea shows the Police Station centre top taking pride of place. The picture on the left shows the rather modest front door to the courtroom off Railway Crescent, whilst the picture to the right shows the covered way from the Police premises to the courtroom via a back door.

These premises seem to have been a combination of schemes from the original Police Station and Court House built in 1898 which was later subject to alterations. In 1937 plans were passed and a contract arranged *'for erection of a new court house at Withernsea and alterations to the existing police station'*.

Although the author does not have sight of the plans of the original premises, it seems likely that the large building to the left of the top picture was an original courtroom, being superseded by the modern one in the 1937 extensions.

The courts were used on a weekly basis on Tuesdays, with a combined Family and Youth Court on every fourth Friday, until 2001 when it was deemed that all Holderness business be transferred to Hull. Since then the court premises have lain idle in that regard. In 2009 the site was being offered for sale for development.

Leven

The Police Station and Court House which were built in 1852 on High Stile were well provided for at the time, as both a witness room and ante rooms were included, both being somewhat of a rarity in those days.

It served as the Petty Sessions venue for the division of North Holderness, which included Arnold and North Skirlaugh; Atwick, Skirlington and Arram; Bewholme and Nunkeeling; Bonwick, Brandesburton, Catfoss, Catwick, Dringhoe, Dunnington, Goxhill, Hatfield Magna, Hatfield Parva, Hempholme, Hornsea, Leven, Mappleton and Rowlston, Moortown, Rise, Riston, Routh, Sigglesthorne, Skipsea, Wassand and Seaton, and Withernwick.

Leven Courthouse.
Picture taken and shown by courtesy of St John Pilkington.

It is recorded that the accommodation included, as well as the courtroom, a magistrates room, witness and ante-rooms, three cells, as well as an apartment for the inspector. The latter was supported by a sergeant, plus three or four constables.

The magistrates for the North Division of Holderness held the sessions here fortnightly, on Wednesdays.

In 1923 when justices started to sit in Hornsea the work was split between Leven and Hornsea on alternative sessions and this continued until 1951 when court work ceased to be held at Leven.

In 2001, on the further reductions in court premises, Hornsea was closed and, although much of its case load was transferred to the courthouse in Bridlington when the new courthouse was built, it is said that work which had been taken from Leven area in former years was passed down to Beverley.

Patrington

T Bulmer s *History and Directory of East Yorkshire, 1892* records that the Petty Sessions for the South Holderness division were held in the court room, which was accompanied on site with cells and residential accommodation for the police inspector, much as for the other premises in the Riding.

Patrington Police Station and Courthouse - 2009.
Picture by the author by courtesy of Andreya and Kevin Young.

However, by 1901 the new court house at Withernsea had been constructed and had taken the action and so Patrington premises were no longer used for the Sessions.

In 2009, when visited by the author, they were in the process of being sensitively refurbished by the occupiers Andreya and Kevin Young. They should remain for many years as a visual reminder of when justice was seen to be done very locally in the community.

Kingston upon Hull

The city is an ancient one, developing from a small hamlet founded by monks in the 12th century. In 1299 it was granted a Royal Charter as a free borough by Edward 1, hence its full name. It became a main seaport on the East coast and continued to grow in importance and featured much in the history of the country and the various conflicts of the Middle Ages.

In 1440 a further charter made Hull an independent county and borough with a mayor, sheriff and twelve aldermen. Over the next four centuries it was managed by them, acting as magistrates holding sessions dealing with both civil affairs and minor criminal matters. Magistrates in Hull also had an extra and unusual duty of witnessing the signing of contracts which permitted transhipment of committed prisoners to the colonies. These particular orders had to be approved by the higher court of Quarter Sessions.

By the late 18th century Hull had become a fast expanding lively borough of considerable note in the country.

The courts in Hull have been situated in buildings known as the Guildhall but the buildings and sites have changed somewhat since 1333, when one building variously described as a moot hall, common hall or guildhall was the meeting place for the town Mayor and Aldermen. It was located at the southern end of Market Place and survived until the early 19th century, but then being in a poor state of repair was demolished in 1806 making way for the shambles.

Around 1630 a second Guildhall was built somewhat to the north of the hall mentioned above and this is shown in the rather handsome watercolour on the next page. To the left of the picture is the Guildhall, which was elevated on stilts in case of flooding; to the right of the arch is the Guardroom and entry to the gaol, which is the tower like structure behind. There does not appear to have been any concern that the gaol might be affected by flood waters. Shortly after 1800, this Guildhall was demolished to make way for Queen Street.

Hull Old Guildhall circa 1700.
A watercolour painting by T Tindall Wildridge from his book
'Old and New Hull', pubished 1884, shown here
by kind permission of Martin Craven.

In 1805, the house of Alderman Jarratt situated on Lowgate, where the east end of today s Guildhall stands, was bought. It was known as the Mansion House and was used to carry out judicial and administrative duties in the City.

Alderman Jarrett s house in Lowgate was used as the Town Hall 1806-1862.

It was described in 1838 as being plain brick with a courtroom behind and a court of requests.

The picture is from 'Old & New Hull' by T Tindall Wildridge, published in 1884, and shown here by courtesy of Martin Craven.

Baines, in his 1823 Directory, comments that public buildings *'do not display any degree of magnificence nor many traces of antiquity'*, a statement which might have been refuted by citizens. He then refers to a House of Correction in Fetter Lane, and a gaol in Myton Place erected in 1783. He goes on to list a Court of Requests established in 1761, a semi-obsolete Sheriff's Court which was held twice a year, a County Court and a Court of Venire for dealing with civil matters.

Assizes had ceased to be held in Hull in 1794 and the cases were sent to York. Quarter Sessions and the other courts in the early 19th century were being held in the Guildhall.

The Lowgate Town Hall site and surroundings were cleared in 1862 to make way for the new Town Hall, Cuthbert Broderick's excellent building, which finally opened in 1866. The new Town Hall included proper accommodation for the Police and the Petty Sessions as well as for the County Courts. Various other civic functionaries occupied additional offices.

The Cuthbert Broderick Town Hall.
Picture by courtesy of Martin Craven, in his possession.

In 1897 Kingston upon Hull was granted city status and larger premises were deemed to be required. To the west of the Town Hall other land was bought for the present Guildhall and the first parts were built; law court, council chamber and offices were completed in 1907. Cuthbert Broderick, although a Hull citizen was not the architect.

The 1907 Guildhall, viewed from the court end
Picture by courtesy of Martin Craven, in his possession.

The Broderick Town Hall was then demolished and the east end of the new building was built fronting on to Lowgate during 1913-1916. This design was by Sir Edwin Cooper and the name Guildhall was once again applied.

Paul Willmer, a Legal Team Manager in Hull in 2009, states that from around 1900 the courts were held in the Guildhall in Alfred Gelder Street, occupying the ground floor at the western end of the building, together with some upstairs accommodation for offices and the Stipendiary Magistrate. This supports commentary from various sources consulted, and the view of the Guildhall West end is shown above.

We must now turn back some years into the 19th century as it is evident that magistrates courts were mainly held for some time not in the Guildhall. The practice presumably commenced when the Municipal Corporations Act divided council duties from legal work.

The 1845 Return of Petty Sessions names The Public Hall in Sculcoates as the venue for the justices, the Clerk being Charles Fox of Hull. Matters taken there were for the Division of South Hunsley Beacon and part of Middle Holderness. The Commissioners of Sculcoates, who owned the building, granted free use to the justices.

There is no mention in the 1845 Return of any courts being held in Hull itself, only those in Sculcoates. It would appear that the Sculcoates building must have been the venue for the justices courts between 1830 and 1862, although some notes of those times mention some court premises situated at the rear of the Mansion House.

The Sculcoates Hall had been built in the 18th century and in the next half-century it had been improved. The Victoria County History Volume 1, published by Oxford University Press remarks *"The Hall, which stood on Jarrett Street, housed the Petty Sessions"*.

In rather more detail, in J J Sheehan s 1866 History of the Town and Port of Hull it notes

"Sculcoates Hall, Worship Street – Before the parish of Sculcoates formed part of the Borough of Hull, this building was erected for, and used as a Sessions House by the Magistrates of the Hunsley Beacon of the East Riding. Soon after the formation of The General Body of Health that body purchased the building of the Sculcoates Commissioners for regulating the affairs of that parish. The edifice, which joins the Public Rooms, is large and of red brick with stone dressings. The entrance is through a recessed portico with four Doric pillars, and the top of the building is parapeted. The first floor is reached by a stone staircase. The room in which the Petty Sessions were formerly held is a fine apartment. The old seal of the Sculcoates Commissioners exhibits a view of the front of this hall, and bears the date 1801".

Baines makes reference to petty sessions being held in the hall and *'Jonas Brown Esq., as the only resident magistrate'*, although others *'from the East-Riding magistrates attend weekly'*. Baines also remarks in 1823 that by then the towns of Sculcoates and Hull had become almost indistinguishable from each other. In 1837 the parish of Sculcoates was absorbed into the borough of Hull.

Sheehan also mentions that in 1866 *"Petty Sessions are held daily in the Police Court. The Borough Justices formerly presided in this Court, but, at the instance of the Town Council, a Stipendiary Police Magistrate (T. H. Travis Esq.,) was appointed by the Crown in 1854"*.

Finally, the fate of the building was sealed in 1886 when a fire brigade of nine men was formed within the police force, and the Sculcoates Hall in Worship Street was acquired for the station and alterations were made to suit its purpose as the fire station for the new Police Fire Brigade.

Plans for this conversion exist in the Hull City Archives and as noted by Dr David Neave in his communications with the author .
"show that the building (still) standing in 1921 was the original Sculcoates Hall with the facade fronting Jarratt Street refronted and broken through with four entrances for the engines and the right hand end section on the Worship Street elevation also converted to engine house". The building was demolished in the 1920s and replaced with a new building which is in present day use.

Sadly, to date no pictures of the original Sculcoates Hall have come to light, but the one below shows the 1890s fire station as converted from the hall; the basic format of the hall was preserved, albeit with the alterations for the convenience of the fire services.

Picture of Sculcoates Hall after conversion to Fire Station.
By kind courtesy of Paul Gibson, www.paul-gibson.com.

At this point we now return to our earlier narrative which ended two pages ago with the completion of Cooper s Guildhall where his fine east frontage replaced the former equally notable work of Broderick. The courts in this building, at the far West end, had the task of containing the court work throughout the 20th century and would have got particularly cramped with all the additional casework which developed in the second half of that century.

In the 1980s, in the former Custom Exchange Building on Lowgate and Alfred Gelder Street, accommodation was made available for three courtrooms to provide for Family and Youth Courts.

The Custom Exchange Building.

This was built 1865-6 adjoining Lowgate and Bowlalley Lane by William Botterill for the Hull Exchange Company.

Picture by Steve Rock 2011.

However, all this diversification was telescoped together in 2001 into the new premises on Market Place. Various outlying courts from Withernsea and Sproatley were closed and the work transferred to Hull.

Hull Magistrates Courts 2010.
By kind courtesy of Paul Gibson, www.paul-gibson.com

FIVE

South Yorkshire

Mainly born out of the old West Riding this county was an entirely new invention resulting from the 1974 boundary reviews. The four boroughs drawn from the Riding in order to create the new county were Barnsley, Rotherham, Doncaster and of course the city of Sheffield. The representative map below indicates just how South Yorkshire was generally cut from the old West Riding.

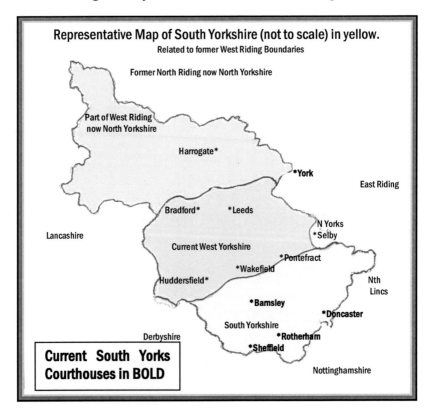

Representative Map of South Yorkshire (not to scale) in yellow.
Related to former West Riding Boundaries

Most of the other smaller towns were the products of the era of coal, albeit perhaps not their originations, and the developments of the mining industry blackened so much of the southern area of the West Riding, not just with the coal itself but with all the other heavy industries which developed from the industrial revolution until the 20th century.

However, by the year 2000 a complete change had come over the area, and parts which had been lost to dust and grime for 150 years have blossomed anew, showing the original beauty of the landscape in all its glory.

As with the other Ridings, the greater part of the area had been set up with several urban or rural district councils around the other boroughs in the county area. In some of these districts were court rooms allied to some parts of administrative buildings.

The wapentakes from former times in the West Riding which formed a large part of new South Yorkshire were Upper and Lower Strafforth and Tickhill, with parts of Staincross and Osgoldcross.

Although not so prolific as in the more northerly parts of the former West Riding, there were more courts held than currently. Just as in other counties the smaller court units were closed as a result of the boundary changes and the ongoing revisions to the administration of justice. The following is a list of those places where sessions took place in 1854.

Barnsley, Bawtry, Doncaster, Hatfield, Thorne, Rotherham, Sheffield, and in addition there is a record of Swinton being another venue.

Let us look into some of these in a bit more detail.

Sheffield

Sheffield is the predominant city of South Yorkshire county and as such it has attracted a major share of the law and order activity in the area. The ancient association with the Hallamshire district of which the city has been a part from Anglo Saxon times adds to its importance, as to many people the city is mainly associated with the rise of steel manufacture during the industrial revolution.

By kind courtesy of Sheffield Archives and the Director of Culture, Sheffield City Council, here follows some extract(s) from the Introduction to Sheffield Archives Court Records catalogue,

"When Sheffield received its charter of incorporation as a borough in 1843 it did not receive its own Commission of the Peace at the same time. This was probably due to the fact that it had refused, on financial grounds, to petition for a Court of Quarter Sessions and a Recorder at the time. Thus, for the time being, magistrates acting in the town of Sheffield did so by virtue of the West Riding Commission of the Peace.

Though Sheffield was not granted its own Court of Quarter Sessions until 1880, a separate Commission of the Peace was granted in 1848. Unfortunately, the early registers for this period do not appear to have survived.

The sessions for the borough and city of Sheffield were held daily, Monday to Saturday, at the Court House, Castle Street (formerly the Town Hall).

Together with registers for the borough and city of Sheffield there are the registers of the Upper Strafforth and Tickhill Division of the West Riding Magistrates. Their jurisdiction lay with cases arising outside the borough boundaries, yet within the Upper Strafforth and Tickhill Division (Sheffield Division). Thus, these registers deal with cases arising in Handsworth, Ecclesfield, and Bradfield etc. Sittings for this court were held separately from the borough magistrates in court No.3. The registers for the court are thus headed No. 3 Register".

"Section III of the Children Act 1908 had established the principle that the hearing of charges against children and young persons should be conducted in a different room or building from where the normal sessions were held, or on a different day (the object being to remove children from associating with the criminal classes). From 1917, a separate series of registers for juvenile sessions begins. The sessions were held at the Coroner's Court in Nursery Street.

The City of Sheffield Commission of the Peace ceased to exist on 1st April 1974 and was replaced by the Commission of the Peace for South Yorkshire.

The registers include the wide range of petty offences. Also included are the records of special sessions for the transfer of beerhouse and licensed victuallers licences, as well as registers of places of detention and other matters .

With regard to liquor, an Act of 1828 had consolidated the law as to the granting by justices of licences to inns, ale-houses and victualling houses. However, as far as beer was concerned, the permissive legislation of 1830 superseded the earlier Act. The 1830 Act, which had been greatly influenced by the free trade thinkers, allowed any householder to take out an excise licence. Though the hours for permitted sale were prescribed, justices were deprived of powers, except in the event of a riot, to order the closure of a beerhouse.

It was not until 1869 that pressure from the growing temperance movement affected the principle of free trade in beer. The Wine and Beerhouse Act of 1869 provided that licences for beer, cider and wine should be granted under the 1828 Act. Thus an applicant could not obtain an excise licence until he had previously obtained a justice's licence. An Act of 1870 continued and extended the 1869 Act, and an Act of 1872 provided that the grant of a new licence by justices must be confirmed by a standing committee of quarter sessions".

Further information, described as below, indicates that other venues, including the Cutlers Hall and various notable houses would have served as premises for taking courts, this being quite common place in those earlier times.

The picture to the left, at times referred to as the Old Cutlers Inn, shows the first Cutlers Hall which was built in 1638 and remained in use until 1725.

Cutlers Hall circa 17th Century.
Courtesy of the Company of Cutlers in Hallamshire.

The building shown to the right was the second Hall in Church Street which was opened in 1725 and which remained in use until 1834.

The Second Cutlers Hall.
Courtesy of the Company of Cutlers in Hallamshire

The practice of holding courts in the Cutlers Hall would by then have ceased as the Town Halls had come into use, as is also noted below.

I am also greatly obliged to John Richman, previously Clerk to the Justices in Sheffield, who has kindly provided some first hand information which is worth quoting *verbatim* from his own notes.

"Between medieval times and 1808, court sessions were held in various places. The Town Hall's predecessor stood at the parish

church gates (today's Sheffield Cathedral), and was by all accounts a fairly ramshackle place, used by the manorial courts as well. In the late 18th century local justice comprised the local vicar, James Wilkinson, of Broom Hall (incidentally still standing and recently owned by the late David Mellor the silversmith), and Col. Robert Athorpe of Dinnington.

Wilkinson was not popular: he bought up a lot of one time common land in the wake of the Enclosure Acts and mobs retaliated by setting Broom Hall on fire. He had been known to put a little girl in the stocks for singing out a popular rhyme celebrating the Broom Hall fire, and for putting a warring husband and wife in the cells with instructions to release them only when they banged on the door and said they had made up their differences.

Col. Athorpe was similarly not universally loved: in the course of one public disturbance in 1795 he ordered military intervention leading to a loss of life: a miniature Peterloo.

Courts were also held in the Cutler's Hall, the first of these was built in 1638 across the road from the parish church. Various great houses all had their justice rooms, including Broom Hall, Clough House at Masborough, The Oakes at Norton, as well as upstairs in the Bagshaw Arms".

"The Sheffield Court House I went to as Deputy Clerk in 1964 and then Clerk in 1969 was originally the Town Hall. This had been built in 1808 by the Town Trustees. At that time they were the nearest thing Sheffield had to a corporation.

They derived their authority and original funds from a charter of Thomas Lord Furnival dated 1297. Their chairman was called the Town Regent or Town Collector. The present incumbent (for they still distribute funds) is my good friend Col. Roger Inman, sometime Chairman of the Sheffield Justices.

The town of Sheffield obtained its charter of incorporation in 1843. By 1897 the Council had built a palatial new town hall at the end of Fargate. The Town Trustees agreed that the name 'Town Hall' be given to this building, and that the old Town Hall be called the 'Court House'. The Duke of Norfolk (who owned much of the freehold of Sheffield and who was also Lord Mayor for two terms around then) was instrumental in adding a splendid new court room to the old building as well as a cell block. By 1900 Sheffield had become a city.

In 1848 Sheffield obtained its first Commission of the Peace. Until then its justices were the West Riding of Yorkshire Commission. Even after 1848 one of the West Riding Divisions, Strafforth and Tickhill Upper, with its West Yorkshire justices, continued to sit at the Court House, as did some West Riding Quarter Sessions. Sheffield did not obtain its own Quarter Sessions and Recorder until 1880. In 1955 Sheffield became an Assize town, and for the purpose the old Court House was enlarged.

In 1945, due to war damage, the Juvenile Courts had to sit in the Coroner's Building in Nursery Street, and some adult courts were held in a chapel on Nursery Street.

In 1974 in the wake of local government reform, the Sheffield City and West Riding Commissions of the Peace ceased, and a new South Yorkshire Commission was created. The old Strafford and Tickhill Division was absorbed into the new Sheffield Division: similar arrangements affected Barnsley, Rotherham and Doncaster. These arrangements survived the demise of South Yorkshire as a local government entity a few years later.

By then the old building was no longer adequate for its purpose, especially with the coming of the Crown Courts. Plans were drawn up and a new magistrates court built and opened in 1979. The Crown Court continued to hold its sessions in the old building for several more years until it in turn moved to a new building. Since then the old Court House, part Grade II listed I believe, has stood empty.

The Court House stands on the corner of Castle Street and Waingate, a little above Lady's Bridge (named from a one-time medieval chapel) over the River Don.

This is the original historic centre where Sheffield Castle stood, home to the Earls of Shrewsbury who had custody of Mary Queen of Scots here from 1570 to 1584. An earlier occupant of this strategic site in Saxon times was possibly Earl Waltheof, so there has *been law and administration and justice of various sorts here for a millennium and more".*

Sheffield Old Town Hall, Waingate.
This is the 1808 building known as The Court House
Picture by kind courtesy of the Yorkshire Post, Johnston Press, 2009.

Sheffield Town Hall, Fargate, completed 1897.
Picture from a private collection.

Not taken on the brightest of March days in 2010, but this view of the working elevation and entrance to the Magistrates Courts illustrates the late 20th century utilitarian approach to civic buildings, in a rather sharp contrast to that of the 19th century, when grandeur was the order of the day.

Sheffield Courts 20th century version.
Picture taken and shown by courtesy of J C Henecka.

In this piece about Sheffield I am grateful for the contributions from the sources named, which bring to life the history of the courts so much more eloquently than this author s contrived narrative. It is help like this from so many kind people which has made the tour through the Yorkshire courts so pleasant.

Those extracts provide a good summary of the arrangements which came into being when the legislation for providing Magistrates courts was enacted in 1830-1840, and the proliferation of the rather grand Town Halls which were built during the 19th century, as various boroughs were incorporated throughout the county and the country, the West Riding being no exception.

Barnsley

Without delving right back in history, as with so many other towns the early dispensing of law was a task undertaken in a Moot Hall, and in the case of Barnsley the record seems to show that such premises were in existence at least in the time of Edward II, almost certainly from the 14th century.

By the early part of the 15th century it was in such a state of disrepair as to require considerable repairs. This matter is referred to in an interesting book *The Vanishing Relics of Barnsley* written by a local historian, Gerald J Alliott. It was not until 1680 that a new Moot Hall was built on a site at the top of Market Hill.

Barnsley Moot Hall.
Drawing by Ron Wilkinson (Wharncliffe Publishing).
Produced here by courtesy of Mr G J Alliott from his book
'The Vanishing Relics of Barnsley'.

The first floor housed the court room, and as was the custom of those times the premises on the ground floor were given over to traders. The Quarter Sessions were held in the Hall which survived until a final session on 4th October 1794, when Frances Edmonds of Worsborough Hall presided. The building was later demolished. Gerald Alliott mentions that a Coat of Arms of Charles II which had adorned the Hall at some time was discovered in a solicitor s office in 1948 and this was sent to Cannon Hall Museum for restoration.

The Moot Hall had a cell beneath and the stocks and a pillory were adjacent to the building so most of the items for dealing with summary justice were to hand. This and other cells in the town were known locally as Grates and it was later near the site of one that an Overseers Office on St Mary s Place was used for quite a while as a court building.

St Mary's Place Overseers Office.
Demolished 1902.
Picture by kind permission of Barnsley MBC Archives and Local Studies.

The Overseers Office had been built on the site of the old Top Grate Prison and adjacent to the Union Workhouse. Viewed from St Mary s Place with the 1879 premises behind, the 1834 Town Hall and Court complex was on its left and to the right it would have butted up to the present Town Hall. The cells in the building were two areas made up from a partitioned storeroom.

The Overseers Office served as a court for some years after the closure of the Moot Hall and before the 1834 premises were built.

Also, it is reported that actual Quarter Sessions were held at the White Bear, later named the Royal Hotel after a visit to the town in 1835 by the then Princess Victoria. Justice being dealt with in local inns was of course quite common in those days, and other examples are mentioned in this book.

Formerly as the White Bear, later as the Royal, the inn served as a courthouse after the Moot Hall ceased to be used in 1794.

Author's picture.

However in 1834 on the 25th September a new Town Hall and Courthouse was opened, all complete with cells and a police station and this then served the town. This fine building was built on the corner of St Mary Gate and St Mary s Place.

An extract from the Petty Sessions Report made to the House of Commons on 19th March 1845 states that Barnsley Court House was . *"A good and substantial well erected building, consisting of a large room, containing in length, 40 feet and 6 inches, in breadth, 25 feet, and in height, 18 feet and 6 inches, with magistrates' private room at one end thereof, and the clerk's room at the other, and a gallery over the magistrates' room, and entrance immediately behind the bench, with two small prisons under the same, and a house, cellar, kitchen, and two chambers attached, in which the matron of the workhouse resides, and has the care thereof, and described as The Court House, all severally being vested in the overseers of the poor of Barnsley for the time being; erected in the year 1833, at the cost of 1,300L, 800L of which was raised by subscription in the district, and 500L paid out of the poor rates for the township of Barnsley".*

This report was of the Upper & Lower divisions of Staincross wapentake and the Clerk was Thomas Marshall of Barnsley.

The 1834 Court House and Town Hall.
Picture by kind permission of
Barnsley MBC Archives and Local Studies.

This view in 1964 was just prior to demolition. By then the Magistrates courts were being held in the 1879 premises and this building was simply known as the police station and it had a link by gantry to the house on the left of the picture.

This was then the main venue for cases to be taken for some years by what would be the West Riding Magistrates for the whole of the district in and around the Barnsley area. The main prison for the town and police station were situated at the other side of St Mary s Place adjacent to Westgate.

Matters did not stop there, as in 1879 a further development took place when the new West Riding Courthouse, together with a Police Station, was built at the junction of Westgate and St Mary s Place. This is shown on the next page.

This proved popular with the prisoners as they were housed adjacent to the courtroom and saved from the ribald abuse which they had suffered when being walked through town from the cells in the

1834 Town Hall. Such must have been their fate in Barnsley for many generations with the system of grates in the town.

The 1879 West Riding Courthouse.
Author's picture.

Alterations took place to the Town Hall in 1901, when it was made over to being a police station with improved accommodation to make it more convenient to house the local prisoners. It would seem that after the creation of the Barnsley County Borough in 1913 any local town magistrates must have sat on an alternating basis with their county colleagues in the 1879 West Riding Courthouse.

It was then in the 1960-70s when a whole new complex of Magistrates Courts, Police Station and Cells were constructed.

The typically 1960-70s soul-less and practical construction which currently serves as the Barnsley Magistrates courthouse.
Author's picture.

This was on a site known as Churchfields between Westgate and Crossfields and which is the present centre of justice.

The first premises on site were those for the police built in the 1960s. The new courthouse as shown above opened in 1974.

Of course the 1974 Boundary Commission changes to local authorities brought about consolidation of West Riding and Borough courts; Barnsley became part of the new South Yorkshire County.

This 20th century courthouse has been brought up to date in the last decade and remains in operation.

For completeness it should be mentioned that there had been a County Court at the bottom of Regent Street and in 1871 the Railway Company took possession of it to provide a new railway station, and by way of compensation provided the funds to build a new County Court on the same street which opened for business in 1872.

Neither of these buildings was used by the magistrates so they are not featured here. The former courthouse which had been acquired by the railway company is now occupied as licensed premises known as The Courthouse Station .

The author is grateful to Barnsley Family History Society and Gerald J Alliott in particular, who has been extremely kind in putting up with so many questions, that matters are so well documented.

Rotherham

The 20th century impression of Rotherham to all but residents will be one of an industrial town belching out the smoke and detritus of a heavy steel industry.

This picture of Rotherham Town Hall showing it in 1700 has a pleasant market place such as was common across the country, and a cobbled area in the foreground showing off a fine building with the design and format of a traditional Moot Hall; seemingly a world away from the bustling town which remains with the trappings of a two centuries of development following the industrial revolution. Any courts would no doubt be held in a room on the upper floor.

Rotherham Old Town Hall.

Picture by courtesy of
Rotherham Archives and Local Studies Service.

Curiously, despite the presence of this magnificent building Baines in his 1822 work makes no reference to it, although he dwells almost extensively on the schools, library churches and other places of architectural or educational merit.

As with many other former West Riding boroughs there was a two courthouse system established in the 19th century; one for the borough business and a second tier to cover the outlying areas of the Riding.

The 1854 return states quite simply that the court business was dealt with in a *'Courthouse, the property of the West Riding'*.

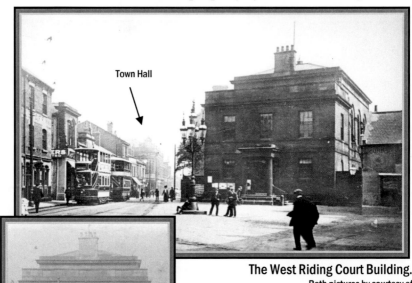

The West Riding Court Building.
Both pictures by courtesy of
Rotherham Archives and Local Studies Service.

An older view of the frontage.

The picture above, from 1904, in the right foreground shows, facing College Square, the former West Riding Courts premises; built in 1828 as a sound 19th century building, as were others of the period.

To the left centre of the picture down Effingham Street there is the Town Hall on which can just be seen the flagpole atop a triangular pediment. This housed the town council as well as the police and borough courts. The courthouse entrance lay on the Frederick Street side of the Town Hall, and this is depicted below.

The premises housed the Rotherham Council Chambers, the Police, the Courts, the Assembly Rooms and Mayoral Suite, which closed for those purposes in 1974. The once beautiful wrought iron staircase to the Mayoral Suite has long been removed, leaving a very nice floor mosaic rendering of the original Rotherham Borough Coat of Arms showing the cannon motif of the local Walker family, the famous makers of cannon used on HMS Victory at the Battle of Trafalgar. The building in 2009 housed a small shopping centre.

The old Rotherham Town Hall in Frederick Street, showing the police entrance on the left and the courts entrance to the right.

Picture taken by G C Smith.

The ongoing effect of the boundary changes in 1974 meant that the former West Riding Council Office building on Moorgate Street, which included police station and courts, became available and the magistrates courts moved into them.

However, after even more changes these very imposing premises which are shown overleaf now act as Rotherham Town Hall with the associated council offices.

Former West Riding Council, Police and Courts building on Moorgate Street
Both pictures taken by G C Smith

On the left is a very interesting interpretation of the Scales of Justice depicted in the old
West Riding Courthouse,
now the Town Hall, above.

However this new Town Hall in Moorgate Street no longer houses the courts, as new Law Courts and Police Station were built on Main Street, all in accordance with modern requirements and they were opened in June 1995, when the justices moved again to these brand new state of the art premises.

Thus, within a period of twenty-one years the original two sets of magistrates, those for the Borough of Rotherham and others from the former West Riding which had served the wider community outside Rotherham, were joined together as one, and they moved their seat of justice twice in that same period of time.

Two views of the new Rotherham Law Courts, the top one showing the huge Coat of Arms set out in coloured bricks.
Pictures by G C Smith.

As at the date of writing, 2009, there do not appear to be any plans to disturb the *status quo*.

Swinton

Not a courthouse of recent times, but it is worth recording that matters of justice were undertaken in Swinton in former years.

Swinton House was the venue; the picture below showing it as it is today, being used as a social club. The stonework is showing its age but otherwise the building is in good condition.

Swinton House.
The plaque to the right reads ....
"Swinton House, 18th Century magistrate's house and jail."

Pictures taken by G C Smith

Local accountant Giles Brearley, who has written *A History of Swinton Hall and Swinton House,* in his helpful letter to the author, remarks that a gentleman called Henry Otter, who owned both of the premises, was also the local magistrate and would have taken some minor cases. It is not clear over what period this usage extended or just when it ceased to be a facility for local justice.

In the house are some cellars and one of these was made into a cell for any serious miscreants who had to be held until they could be taken to Rotherham or York for trial.

Giles Brearley also writes, *I did discover that coroner's courts were conducted in the local pubs in Swinton and Mexborough for miners killed underground during this period. At one of the Warren Vale Colliery explosions an inquest was held at the Sportsman Inn, Fitzwilliam Street, Swinton."*

Swinton is another place in the county where local justice was administered by the local magistrate, as is evidenced in many of the other items which make up this record of past and present seats of justice.

Doncaster

On the main Roman road to the North, Doncaster has always been a significant location. In 1194 a town charter was granted by the King and a traditional Moot Hall served the community. In 1248 a charter was granted for Doncaster Market to be held around the Church of St Mary Magdalene. It also seems that the Moot Hall was in the grounds of the church and was later developed into the Town Hall.

Old Church of St Mary Magdalene.
This was used as the Town Hall, until being demolished as shown in 1846.

From a lithograph in "St Mary Magdalene" by the Rev John Jackson published in 1853.

A borough charter of 1467 was responsible for the creation of a mayor coroner and as a solitary justice of the peace, but a further charter in 1505 enabled three aldermen to be justices with additional independence for the latter to sit apart from the West Riding Justices. Further Acts in later years developed the legal divisions which led to county courts, but these are not the subject of this book.

Philip Langford of the Doncaster Archaeological & Historical Society kindly offers this commentary extract from the paper which he prepared for the Society on the Town Hall   .   *It developed from the church of St Mary Magdalene. The age of that church is not known but evidence suggests that it was possibly Saxon. It was replaced as the parish church by St George's about 1200. At the*

Dissolution of the Chantry chapels in 1548 the entire property including graveyard became Crown property. The Church with its cemetery was sold by the Crown to Thomas Reve and George Cotton of London in 1548. In 1552 they sold it to Ralph Bossvile and in February 1556 Bossvile sold it to John Symkynson a mercer of Doncaster who had been mayor in 1547. Then in 1557 Symkynson sold it to the Mayor and Corporation who instead of demolishing the chapel refitted the old chancel as a grammar school and started converting the rest for the use as the Borough meeting house. In 1575 the north & south aisles were taken down and during the 1700's it was made to look like a Georgian building. By the 1840's more space was needed for market expansion and in 1846 the Town Hall was demolished. Some of the old church was found inside".

The Old Town Hall on the left.   **The Theatre to the right.**
Courtesy of Doncaster Library Service Archives.

Baines, in his 1823 work, remarks that the Town Hall had been *'repaired and beautified'* in 1784 and *'further elevated in 1805'*.

It housed a Court of Requests and the meetings of the Justices *'to transact the business of the district'* are held every Saturday.

He notes that the Corporation of Doncaster included a Mayor, Recorder, Town Clerk and 12 Aldermen, of whom three senior were *'invested with the authority of Justices of the Peace'*, plus 24 Common Councilmen.

The Petty Session Return to Parliament of 1845 reports that Courts for Lower Strafforth and Tickhill Division were held in the Town Hall, *'where general Quarter sessions are held';* the clerk making the return being Geo Crawshaw. No charge was made for the use of the premises. This must have been one of the last reported sessions prior to the demolition in the following year.

Eric Jackson in his book on the Pontefract Sessions house quotes an Act of Parliament, (46 Geo.III 1806) being: ...

.... *"An Act to enable the Justices of the Peace for the West Riding of the County of York to provide convenient court houses for holding the General Quarter Sessions of the Peace within the said Riding* . This Act enabled the Justices to *erect, build or otherwise provide...proper courthouses* in Wetherby, Wakefield, Doncaster, Pontefract, Skipton, Bradford, Rotherham, Knaresbrough, Leeds, Sheffield and Barnsley*; Whereas the court houses or buildings in the said towns...are for the most part very ancient buildings greatly out of repair* .

The Guildhall was built in 1847 on the site of the Old Angel, Frenchgate, opening in 1848. It is not known where courts were held from 1846-48 but the comments below may throw light on the matter.

The Guildhall.
Courtesy of Doncaster Library Service Archives.

The Mansion House had been built in 1747, but there are various queries as to whether it was used for court purposes or other than a fine ceremonial establishment for the Mayor and Corporation.

Information posted on a Doncaster Council website describing the Mansion House tour makes mention as follows;

"The ground floor of the Mansion House contains several rooms whose purpose was severely practical. To the left of the front door lie the two committee rooms", making reference to *Probably this room was originally used for the twice-weekly magistrates court for the borough"*...adding...

Paine's published plans give no indication of the use of these rooms on the ground floor. However, in Doncaster Archives there are volumes of Mansion House inventories dating from 1756 to 1908. These allow us to discover the use to which the rooms were put and how they were furnished. They show that the Mansion House, besides being a place for civic entertainment, was used for local government purposes from the beginning. In the mid-eighteenth century, the ground floor housed the grandly-titled 'court of judicature' (where the mayor and his three fellow aldermen - magistrates held a magistrates court every Monday morning), a councillors' room, an aldermen's room and a gentlemen's dining room".

So much for the Mansion House in this story. The Guildhall was demolished during 1969, shortly after the new courts opened.

The 19th century saw additional regulations which developed Petty Sessions separately for the Borough and for the West Riding, albeit that both sat in the town in different venues.

This brought about the erection of a Police Station combined with court room facilities, shown in the next picture, situated on Old Station Road.

The premises seem to have been opened in late 1899 as it is not recorded in the Doncaster trade directory for 1899 but is there in the 1900 version, which would probably have been prepared late in 1899, so that would seem to indicate it began to function round about the turn of the year.

The West Riding Courthouse.
Courtesy of Doncaster Library Service Archives.

Alongside is a picture of the first court in the West Riding Courthouse, as shown in *The Court is Sitting* written by Ernest W Pettifer, Clerk to The West Riding Justices in Doncaster 1940.

The above mentioned book provides a very interesting story of events around those times and is well worth a search for a copy in old book shops by those who would like to learn more about the courts in those years.

Closure dates are also slightly ill defined, but a letter in the archives from the West Riding Justices Clerk on 14th August 1968 is from Old Station Road, whereas one from the same person on 17th March 1969 is addressed from the new courthouse on College Road.

The date of demolition is not readily available but it does not seem necessary to pursue that point, although nothing is recorded in the Council Planning Committee minutes up to 1974. Even though the courts vacated, the police may have remained in place until later.

The above information has been kindly provided through the good offices of Andrew Young, archivist in the Doncaster Archives.

In addition a court was established at Thorne early in the 19th century, and some other sittings were held in Bawtry. Both of these will be detailed later on in the book.

On 14th March 1969 the new magistrates courts, as mentioned above, were opened by Her Majesty s Attorney General the Rt. Hon. Sir Frederick Elwyn Jones Q.C., M.P. in the presence of the Mayor, W H Kelly Esq., situated on College Road as depicted below in the picture kindly provided to the author by the retiring lady chairman, Anne Roberts, who donated it to the court.

Copy of a painting of the Doncaster Law Courts.
Kindly provided by Anne Roberts who had the work commissioned
by the artist Anthony Knight in her period as Chairman.
The original, which she presented to the Court, hangs in the premises.

Thorne and Bawtry

The 1845 Return to Parliament records that a portion of the Lower Division of Strafforth & Tickhill, which included Thorne and other places, met in a room at the Blue Bell Inn at Hatfield, The Clerk being a gentleman by name of William Lister of Thorne.

In the same year the return for another part of the same division stated that a court was held in Bawtry in the office of William Broughton, a solicitor, as there was no other suitable public room in the town. The returning clerk was a Mr W L Baines. Bawtry never rose in status to merit its own courthouse and its business must have been merged, possibly with Thorne, or directly with Doncaster.

However, later it was deemed that Thorne was big enough to have its own court and the premises which came to be used for that purpose, as in other places, combined police station and courthouse.

Thorne Courthouse and Police Station.
In 2009 only the police remain.
Picture by courtesy of St John Pilkington.

Thorne Courthouse was closed on 31st August 1997. The fine carved court furniture being moved to Doncaster where it furnishes Courtroom 9 in the modern premises.

Journey s End

That concludes this trip through the variety of places where, over a few hundred years in some cases, local peers in communities have stood together or sat in judgement of the behavioural defaulters within their ranks.

Whether by the ancient method of raising their pikes or staves, or after the deliberations of locally appointed justices in more recent times, decisions have been made by the people in the affected areas.

It will by now be evident to any reader that whereas in some places information has been quite comprehensive, in others any record of magisterial activities is less available. Of course, records of cases held in files or microfiche in county archives tell a lot about the types of offences dealt with over the years, but details of the venues in some instances are more difficulty to ascertain. Hopefully, therefore, some who read this attempt to gather this information into one record will be inspired to search around to ensure that this important part of our heritage is retained other than as a distant memory.

Although references are made to earlier historical whereabouts of some courts, the purpose has not been to provide a comprehensive lengthy in depth examination on law enforcement. Such as has been mentioned is merely some background to the later comments on the provision and disposition of courthouses in more recent times.

Consequently, the reader will have noted an inclination on the part of the author to comment on the way perceptions of local justice have changed over the years. There is no doubt that improvements in methods of transportation, by bus, car and train, have changed the make up of local communities. In addition, population expansion has created new towns or communities as adjuncts of others.

In villages there can be two ends, the one populated by owners and the other by tenants. In towns and cities the 1930s starter efforts at slum clearance and post war late 1940s, 50s and 60s areas of council housing injected new communities into them. Whole new towns arose in some places, devouring many acres of countryside and farmland.

Whereas the inter-war estates seemed to be largely respected by grateful occupants who were lifted from squalid backstreets, too many of following generations seem to have been less respectful, with some of the later developments being destined to failure as sink estates. Inconsiderate occupants and consequent indifferent reputation of some areas have made them less than desirable for those wanting a peaceable life.

All of this has affected the way justice has been served within more recent years, together with a growth of administrative structures between defendant, court and community compensation by penalty.

A greater need for secure accommodation or basic safety has decreed the need for the parties to cases being kept apart; no longer is it satisfactory for magistrates to elbow their way past crowds of their future customers to get to their room as they arrive at court, or to sit on the stairs to deliberate on cases. Likewise, witnesses must not be intimidated as they nervously wait their turn. But all things must be equal, even the naughty ones must not be kept in damp dungeons with a bucket in the corner for nervous relief.

Quite rightly this has brought on the provision of new court buildings of varying architectural merit and there are few major cities or towns where this is not the case. To argue that this especially has brought about the destruction of fine old buildings is fallacious, as within this book alone there is plenty of evidence that the providers of so many of our most prestigious civic buildings, the Victorians and related Edwardians, were also amongst the most destructive of our former heritage.

Such as the fine Moot Hall in Leeds which blocked the way for road development bit the dust, whereas the Cathedral, which was an equal obstruction, was moved to a less inconvenient place. Kingston upon Hull had a Town Hall knocked down not over long after being built to be replaced by another. In various other places the wholesale clearance of medieval buildings for development was the order of the day. Much of this change took place after the 19th century Act which regularised the place of the magistrates and divided away the civic control from justices of the peace to what became councils elected by the people.

The late 20th and early 21st century changes have not been unlike as these have reflected shifting populations, but there has been a big addition, this being the growth of back up logistics.

As with so many other centrally controlled state bodies there has developed an overwhelming desire to manage from the centre and the simple process of subverting the position of the Justices Clerk by imposition of a Chief Executive has had wide reaching implications.

There are amongst the legal community those who feel that application of the law has now become subservient to administrative needs and financial restriction, whilst back rooms have been filled with advisors.

Be that as it may, the latest round of court closures announced as the final pages of this record are compiled is almost the last straw for many who have dedicated a large part of their lives to serving the community as justices of the peace. It is typical that this has been dictated by costs, poorly disguised as necessary changes to take into account further security needs or ongoing community shifts.

Already there has been considerable unease at the arbitrary use of ticket penalties imposed by the police or even council employees in the guise of community support officers. Acceptance of such is the easy way to avoid an expensive fight in court but also lands the payer with a criminal record, take it or leave it. As a result the work of the justices has reduced, in big cities as well as lesser places. However, that is no reason for the function of what remains to be further reduced by transposition to far distant places; and in the case of some counties they are indeed many miles away where the option for a banned driver would be a rather long walk in the total absence of public transport.

There could be a solution which would retain the principle of local justice by local justices, especially in rural areas, as well as catering for the more complex cases which would require seriously secure lock-ups and the attendant security staff.

In this, we should recall that justices originally dealt with petty crime, whilst more serious offences were reserved for quarter sessions in appropriate premises. This does not mean that magistrates should be limited to only handling the trivial as those who wish can still be elevated as required to serve on the higher benches. In this case we can, as in so many instances, learn from the past.

Reorganisation of the 1970s saw new county administrative boundaries created and the demise of the Urban and Rural District Councils, many of these being swept into larger Borough units joined to major cities. However, local representation was retained in the form of Parish and Town Councils which kept some ability to manage a few local services to their communities, notably in the rural areas.

Most of the former bodies had council offices, or even town halls which were retained under the new arrangements, the buildings being used for area offices, information centres or such other local purposes as the larger authorities thought fit to disseminate services. In nearly all of these there is a formal council chamber, many being meticulously preserved and used by the parish or town councils for their meetings on a few days per month. Some of these even held the courts in earlier times, until reorganisation took place. Where better to hold court for all such cases which do not require custody suites and are genuinely petty offences in the locality?

Returning so many of the latter from being ticket penalties , which are too widely ignored, would restore some faith in local justice being seen to be done. An element of responsibility for defendants to have to appear in court would also drive home the message to the far too many whose misbehaviour is a tiresome menace to communities.

Usage could be according to need, even if only once per two weeks, the cost being offset by the saving in travel costs to the more distant large courts.

This would also cover the possibility that if local justices can not sit in their locality, they will cease to come forward to serve. That would be a further nail in the coffin of delivery of local justice for local people. To have magistrates drawn only from the citizens of the larger towns, cities or the more populous boroughs would scarcely be representative of all communities.

At a time when politicians are trying to emphasise their desire to reactivate responsibility in local communities, restoration of the concept of local justice by local people would be a positive step.

BIBLIOGRAPHY
AND
ACKNOWLEDGEMENTS

Various sources of information have been mentioned in each of the pieces which make up this book. Each of these has contributed in a specific way as noted in the individual extracts and they are all duly acknowledged with grateful thanks.

However, it will be evident to the reader that much has been forthcoming from certain main documents, these being .

The Return of Petty Sessions to the House of Commons dated 19th of March 1845.

History, Directory and Gazetteer of the County of York, with a variety of commercial, statistical and professional information, also copious lists of the Seats of the Nobility and Gentry of Yorkshire, written by Edward Baines 1822.

Likewise, I am very grateful for that information, especially including David Pybus of Whitby who introduced me to the first of these two publications.

It would be quite wrong for me to list those who have helped in progression, but I must make special mention of Paul Sherwood in North Yorkshire who has done so much investigating and taken so many pictures in those parts.

To add to that Michael Rawnsley, lately Justices Clerk for a large part of North Yorkshire, spent a deal of time relating memories of the period from his youthful qualification in West Yorkshire and in the years thereafter.

In the distant parts of the North East of the traditional county Si n Jones has been m ost helpful in bringing to light facts and figures, checking some copy and introducing me to the valuable book *'Six into one will go'*, an interesting tale of courts and mergers in that area.

In the Holderness area of East Yorkshire a leading light has been Martin Craven, a specialist in that district, and over the wider area of that county Neil Marquis, now retired from the court service, was a great help.

West Yorkshire has benefited from the considerable works of Michael Smelt lately of the Bradford Crown Courts, as well as Marian Griffith and her husband in the Calderdale area. Derek Middleton, also now retired, has been a great provider of matters relating to the complications of the mergers over the years in and around Leeds.

In South Yorkshire my very long standing non-magisterial colleague and friend Geoff Smith has done much to assist, especially in and around his home town of Rotherham and nearby Sheffield. I am also very grateful to the other listed and quoted contributors.

Generally, StJohn Pilkington, whose erudite articles appear in the Magistrate, has been of a great help with his wide knowledge resulting from his own searches. I hope that my efforts to reciprocate have been as worth while to him.

Many of the informers mentioned in the book arose by the inclusion of an article in the Dalesman magazine which Paul Jackson, the editor, was kind enough to publish. This brought forth a useful shower of contacts with helpful information and personal recollection.

Encouragement from Anthony Chadwick and his colleagues at the Courthouse Museum in Ripon, under the chairmanship of Richard Taylor, has been helpful and I hope they will feel that the end product is worthy of their interest in the promotion of their interesting and excellent facilities.

Not the least by any means, my thanks go to all those working in various public services such as libraries and archives who, without exception, have been generous with their help. Their keen willingness at times to find obscure information has been greatly appreciated.

Finally, there is always the possibility that in transposing this information to these pages names or facts may have been mislinked. Should that be the case, my sincere apologies are tendered to those so affected and notification of any such error would be appreciated.

The Courthouse Museum at Ripon

In the book I have referred in several places to the museum and the way it has undertaken the task of re-instating as well as preserving and developing the buildings and artefacts.

The Museum Trust also pursue a series of re-enactments which draw useful crowds to view the way that law and order used to be maintained as well as seeing how those who were destitute were given work and sanctuary in the manner of the times.

As I have explored the county it has become obvious that there is a need for such information not just to be preserved, but to be spread more widely, otherwise we are in danger of losing the memories and forgetting just how social problems, crime and justice walked hand in hand.

It is probably not unfair to say that continues today and it is right that parallels can be drawn so that those in charge of law and order in the country learn from the past and go forward in their efforts to continue to improve the state of affairs in the 21st century.

The museums are more than worth a visit, they are a must do. A visit is recommended to find out more about the story of law and order in Yorkshire.

For more information their website is: www.riponmuseums.co.uk

and they can be contacted at

The Workhouse Museum, Tel: 01765 690799.
75 Allhallowgate
Ripon
North Yorkshire
HG4 1LE

PICTURE ACCREDITATION

I am grateful to all those people who have so kindly provided pictures of court houses, often with additional information, and these are listed below and/or are mentioned within the substantive text. The author has tried diligently to ascertain all sources but apologises for any errors or omissions. Those marked own pictures are either taken by the author or in his possession.

THE YORKSHIRE WAPENTAKES Colin Hinson of Yorkshire CD Books
CHANGING TIMES David C H Hall JP

West Yorkshire

Leeds	Leeds Library and Information Service, Andy Paraskos, The Thoresby Society. Brian Jennings, own pictures.
Morley	Morley Antiquarian Society, Leeds Library & Information Service, The Thoresby Society, Morley Community Archive, own pictures,
Wetherby	Own pictures
Horsforth	Horsforth Museum and own pictures
Rothwell	Councillor Chris Townsley, own picture
Otley	Otley Court House Museum, own pictures
Pudsey	Michael Brookes and own pictures
Bradford	Michael Smelt, City Libraries and Information and Museum and Galleries Service, C H Wood Photographic collection, HMCTS Bradford, Hurdrolland Partnership, Jas England of Carter Jonas
Keighley	Own Pictures
Bingley	Sketches by R A Curry
Slaidburn	Stephen Carter
Queensbury	Derek Paley
Halifax	Malcolm Bull – Calderdale Companion, Michael Smelt, Stephen Gee, Marian and David Griffith, own pictures
Brighouse	David Griffith
Todmorden	David Griffith
Huddersfield	Kirklees Images Archive, own pictures
Holmfirth	Own pictures
Uppermill	Saddleworth Museum Archives, Townswomen's Guild collection.
Dewsbury	Dewsbury Reporter, Kirklees Images Archive, own pictures
Batley	StJohn Pilkington
Wakefield	Kate Taylor, Yorkshire Archaeological Society, own pictures

Ossett	Ossett Historical Society, own pictures
Pontefract	Eric Jackson, own pictures
Wentbridge	Own pictures
Castleford	Ruth Woodhouse, own picture
Wentbridge	Own pictures
Aberford & Sherburn	Own pictures
Tadcaster	Peter Bradshaw, Tadcaster Community Archives, own pictures
Snaith	Own pictures

North Yorkshire

York	Own pictures
Selby	Richard Moore, own pictures
Sedbergh	Own picture
Ingleton	John Bentley, own picture
Settle	Own pictures
Skipton	North Yorks County Council & Mrs V Rowley, own pictures
Pateley Bridge	Nidderdale Museum, own pictures
Ripon	Own pictures courtesy of Ripon Museum Trust
Knaresborough	Own pictures, sketch by R A Curry
Harrogate	Malcolm Neesam, Marilyn Stowe, own pictures.
Wath	Paul Sherwood
Leyburn	Paul Sherwood
Muker	John Severs and Paul Sherwood courtesy of John Kilburn
Aldborough	David Lorimer
Tockwith	John Graham
Bedale	Paul Sherwood
Scorton	Paul Sherwood
Richmond	Paul Sherwood
Easingwold	Sheila Jefferson, courtesy of Paul Sherwood, Michael Riley
Crayke	Michael Ibbotson
Helmsley	Paul Sherwood
Thirsk	Paul Sherwood
Northallerton	Colin Narramore, Paul Sherwood, Northallerton Camera Club, N Yorkshire County Records Office, Richard Jennison
Greta Bridge	Paul Sherwood
Malton & Norton	John Stone, own pictures
Flaxton	Own picture
Kirkbymoorside	Robin Butler courtesy of and with others by Louise Mudd.
Pickering	The Beck Isle Museum Trust and Mrs Barbara Sokel, author

Whitby	Bagshawes, North Yorkshire Law, David Pybus, John Tindall Whitby Literary & Philosophical Society.
Scarborough	Max Payne courtesy of Kevin Page HMCTS, own pictures
Wykeham	Downe Arms courtesy of the Dawnay Estates
Stokesley	Estelle Scott, Peter Wood former owner of Studio Print and Joe Richardson of Stokesley Pride, Paul Sherwood
Guisborough	G C Smith
Loftus	Own picture
Redcar	StJohn Pilkington
Yarm	G C Smith
Southbank	Malcolm Race
Middlesbrough	Roger Robinson plus Thornaby & South Bank etchings

East Yorkshire

Escrick	J P G Taylor
Brough	Neil Marquis
Welton	Own Picture
Howden	Neil Marquis
Goole	Neil Marquis and own pictures
Driffield	John Harrison FRICS FAAV
Market Weighton	Enid Geenwood, Neil Marquis
Pocklington	Neil Marquis
Beverley	Neil Marquis, own pictures
Bridlington	Neil Marquis and own pictures
Hornsea	Neil Marquis, Martin Lonsdale
Hedon	Own pictures taken by courtesy of Martin Craven and Hedon Town Council
Sproatley	Mark and Sandra Betts and own pictures by their courtesy
Withernsea	Clark Weightman and Company
Leven	StJohn Pilkington
Patrington	Andreya and Kevin Young
Hull	Martin Craven, Paul Gibson www.paul-gibson.com, Steve Rock

SouthYorkshire

Sheffield	Company of Cutlers in Hallamshire, G C Smith, Yorkshire Post Johnston Press, J C Henecka
Barnsley	G J Alliott, Barnsley MDC Archives and Local Studies, own pictures

Rotherham   Rotherham Archives and Local Studies Service, G C Smith
Swinton   G C Smith
Doncaster   Anne Roberts and Doncaster Library Service Archives.
Thorne   StJohn Pilkington

The Lost Courthouses of Yorkshire

For Notes and pictures

The Lost Courthouses of Yorkshire

For Notes and pictures

The Lost Courthouses of Yorkshire

For Notes and pictures

For Notes and pictures